THE IRISH KLONDIKE

Modern Ireland, Migration, Media

A *'deplorable'* perspective

Frank Cosgrove

Contents

Appendices

INTRODUCTION

From the amount of public discussion on the subject, one might conclude that the arrival on our shores in recent times, of large numbers of immigrants, was a matter of supreme indifference to the Irish people. I would beg to differ with those who might be of this opinion. The problem is that those who control and orchestrate public discussion, have allowed their own beliefs and opinions to act as a filter on the views and concerns of the general public. Consequently, the alarm felt by many people at the enormous influx – and it is enormous – finds little or no expression in public discourse.

Even the most cursory examination of the figures indicates the disturbing extent of that prolonged period of, what might be justifiably called mass migration, that occurred here in Ireland during the Celtic Tiger period. Following a dip after the 2008 Crash, immigration into the country has been steadily ramping up since then. Mass migration, of course, is not a term used by the Irish media who, despite the evidence all around us, pretend or seem not to have noticed that anything unusual has happened at all. The most fundamental change in Ireland since the Great Famine is the flood of inward migration that has taken place in the last twenty five years and those whose business it is to report, critically analyse and interpret events great and small, have presumably failed to notice. Not only have they failed to notice, but in a classic case of denial, they seem intent on preventing any meaningful discussion and debate on the negative aspects of this development. They have rounded on those who have had the temerity to express concern or alarm at a demographic shift of enormous proportions, labelling them racists, fascists and xenophobes.

This is an abuse of privilege by the media and it is widespread in Ireland and the West generally. This labelling of those who oppose large-scale immigration as racists is fake news. Racism and opposition to mass migration are two completely different things. Racism is a personal antipathy to persons of a different race. *'The Concise English Dictionary'* defines racism as *'antagonism between different races'*. Opposition to mass migration on the other hand, is a belief that the influx of large numbers of people from elsewhere into a particular place or country should be strictly controlled. The relentless campaign to brand those who hold this perfectly legitimate view as racists, is misleading and simply wrong.

When the Merkel invitation of late summer 2015 unleashed that infamous episode of mass migration into Germany, it was soon acknowledged as such in most quarters, despite a reluctant media. Over a short period almost 1 million people had arrived in Germany. The difference between the Irish and German experiences is that the German episode lasted four months and added 1 per cent to the population – the Irish episode lasted four years (2005-2008) and added almost 7 per cent to our population. Not only that, but in the ten years just before, a further 7 per cent had arrived and very high levels of inward migration continue to this day.

The end result is that today, almost 20 per cent of the population of this country is non-Irish, an ethnic shift unparalleled anywhere in Europe, with the possible exceptions of Switzerland, Austria and Sweden. Unlike in Europe, this has all come about with little or no public debate about its desirability or otherwise. Would any issue of such fundamental social, economic and cultural importance be given so little consideration in any other country? While our media obsess about relatively minor issues, the hugely important ones are ignored. Their eyes are shut firmly against the elephant in the room – the tsunami of immigration.

This fog of confusion about the importance or otherwise of issues in the public mind, is being exploited by highly motivated groups who have managed to hijack the public discourse, or have been granted media space for the promotion of their own agendas, which are invariably of the politically correct variety. These views, given enough exposure and going largely unchallenged in a highly partisan media, soon assume the appearance of fact.

The equality concept with its own supporting industry of rights groups, is the Trojan Horse of political correctness. Political correctness has emerged as a dominant ideology here and in Western societies and is adept at having its agenda adopted at every level of society, with some bizarre results. However, the equality concept does not seem to apply to certain economic issues such as the taxation of the rich or the economic condition of the indigenous poor or indeed, to those awkward social issues like the rights of the unborn or euthanasia.

The ascendancy of 'progressive liberalism' and political correctness is polarising Western societies to a degree not seen since the 1930s. In Ireland, at least a third of the electorate is voiceless in politics and public discourse. They are seen as the backward rump of society, not unlike the Trump supporters, who cling to religion, nationality and tradition, all of which are held in barely concealed contempt by the liberal establishment. They are the people who have been steamrolled out of the way in what Leo Varadkar has termed the 'quiet revolution'. Quiet indeed, because they have been successfully excluded from the public conversation, intimidated, ridiculed and shouted down. The only reason we know that they are still there at all, is that some of them have mustered up the courage to come out and vote against the 'progressive' propositions in recent referenda.

While in other societies objectors to the liberal consensus are more vocal, the Irish tendency to be agreeable, to tell people what they want to hear, conceals their opposition and gives the impression of unanimous support. It remains to be seen how long the consensus on large-scale inward migration can remain intact in Ireland. Events on the European Continent where opposition to large-scale immigration is intensifying may well embolden opposition here. For the moment however, the prohibition on dissent remains firmly in place.

The German migration episode of 2015 unleashed a wave of distrust of the media which has since spread and continues to grow. The phenomenon of 'the lying press' or 'nanny journalism' gained currency when the German media failed to report criminal activity and sexual assaults carried out by recently arrived asylum seekers in Cologne on new year's eve 2016. Numerous similar incidents have since come to light, mainly on the internet and reluctantly, subsequently in the media. The main function of the media to report and analyse facts, is now believed by many to have been overtaken by the desire to spin the facts in the politically correct direction. The journalist is no longer a dispassionate observer but has become a political actor. He has become a liberal champion who must slay the populist dragon, even at the cost of killing free speech. The first fruit of this transformation is the phenomenon of 'fake news'.

The attempt to suppress public discourse on migration is part of this agenda. In Britain and Europe this attempt has failed. A great debate is taking place about the issue and its consequences in the Western world and this is just as it should be. The populist insurgency that has shaken Western politics to its foundations is partly, if not largely, a reaction to large-scale immigration. It has already led to some unsettling political developments for the ruling elites in the West. The debate about migration has not yet, however, manifested itself in Ireland, in either politics or public discussion, despite its huge impact on Irish society.

This may be partly explained by Breda O'Brien's article in *The Irish Times* on the 9th January 2016 [(1)], where she discusses 'the strong conformist streak in the Irish psyche'. She says *'We have replaced one set of authorities we feared to challenge with another, equally strong group that continues to set the boundaries of permissible views'*. Our overwhelming impulse to say 'it's grand', has allowed a pushy, manipulative media to impose their views on Irish society and exclude dissenting voices. Our tendency to be agreeable is a weakness that is taken for acquiescence with, an often toxic consensus.

Within the media itself, there is also a strong conformist streak. The Irish media and indeed Western media in general, are riddled with the phenomenon of group think. Recent examples are the overwhelming support for Hillary Clinton, the opposition to Brexit in the UK media, the defamation of Galway priest Fr. Reynolds in Ireland and indeed the unrelenting campaign against the Catholic Church. There are very few deviations from the liberal free-market consensus in Ireland.

Of course the liberal consensus in the media is reflective of the beliefs of a large section of Irish society. It is the credo of the Irish counterpart of that section of American society that was flummoxed by the Trump victory and the remainers in the Brexit vote. It's the replacement religion for the enlightened, the people whose sense of entitlement was outraged by Trump and Brexit and their 'deplorable' supporters. As is always the case when a new religion appears, a gap soon opens up between those that have seen the light and non-believers. That gap has now become a chasm, running through the heart of US and European society.

The dissenting section of society, who refuse to conform to the new orthodoxy, have found a voice in populist politics, having previously been effectively shut out by the mainstream media. For at least a generation, the liberal progressive tendency has succeeded in keeping the silent minority – if it is indeed a minority –silent, but this seems unlikely to continue for much longer. The battle-ground for the looming confrontation between the liberal elite, their supporters and the rest, is probably going to be the migration issue.

The polarisation of society, so often regretfully alluded to by elements in the media, is a direct result of the deliberate attempt by 'progressive' forces in the establishment, the liberal elite and the media itself, to silence those who disagree with them. They have nothing but contempt for the concerns of ordinary citizens who do not share their view, hence the infamous Clinton designation of 'deplorable'. All those crocodile tears about divisiveness and polarisation stem from the failure of the elite to quell dissent. The problem with polarisation is that it can lead to open warfare in the streets and there are indications that this may already be happening on the margins of Western societies.

The steady advance of populist politics in the Western world today is being carried on the tide of concern regarding immigration. It is the subject at the heart of that great debate in Britain, Europe and the United States. No amount of shouting racist or xenophobe from the moral high ground will quell that debate. Potentially up to one billion people living on a couple of dollars a day in underdeveloped countries would move to the developed world, given half a chance, and who could blame them. That is the equivalent of the entire population of the Western world. In recent years we have seen the leading edge of that potential manifest itself at the gates of Europe and America. With more globalisation, easier faster travel and more resources available to migrants, that flood could become a raging torrent. The migrant bridgeheads that have already been established in cities, towns and villages in Ireland and the Western world, will ease and facilitate increased flows of people from Africa, Asia and elsewhere, just as they have done in the past for Europeans in America.

While the unprecedented episode of mass migration into Germany in 2015 has ended and the flow into southern Europe has eased, this may be just a pause before the beginning of a new phase of migration from the poorer countries into Europe, on a scale never seen before. Even without a spectacular episode like 2015, the continuous steady flow of migrants into Europe and Ireland, that has become the norm, is bringing about an alarming demographic transformation. The cultural, social and economic repercussions of these developments are unknown but are likely to have a considerable negative effect on the less well-off in the receiving countries. The question we must ask ourselves is whether the prosperity, stability and the social cohesion of Europe is worth sacrificing on the altar of political correctness?

While the debate on this question is convulsing every country in Europe and shaking politics and societies to their very foundations, Ireland sleepwalks on the edge of a demographic precipice. In Ireland, where the immigration phenomenon exceeds almost all our neighbours, it is not acceptable to critically examine, discuss or debate this issue. In Britain, with considerably lower per capita immigration than here, concern about this issue has helped to bring about the political earthquake of Brexit. Meanwhile, Ireland − near the top of the European immigration league table − is as calm as a mill pond. None of the many political parties in Dail Eireann dare mention the 'migration' word, for fear of drawing down upon themselves the wrath of the politically correct 'progressive' elite and their servants and supporters. The immigration issue has shifted the political centre of gravity in Europe decidedly to a more identity, community centred direction, while we in Ireland, with a considerably larger 'problem', are moving in the opposite direction. Many Europeans have come to the conclusion that large-scale inward migration poses a threat to their way of life and must be strictly controlled.

If our culture, identity, traditions and values – and indeed our economic structures, including the welfare state – are worth preserving, we must carefully consider whether or not we are prepared to allow uncontrolled immigration to erode or seriously damage what has been painstakingly built up over the last hundred years. Discussion and debate is a key part of the process of deciding what to do. We cannot allow some self-appointed elite to make this decision for us. The idea that the most important issue of the day, which has brought about massive political change elsewhere has been declared taboo by a dictatorship of the commentariat in Ireland, is outrageous and unacceptable.

This book attempts – in the absence of those who might be better qualified – to discuss the changes and effects of immigration on Ireland and its people, from the perspective of an ordinary 'deplorable', as Hillary Clinton elegantly put it. It is not an academic treatise or the work of a trained researcher. It is the view from the little known perspective of the taxpaying citizen who stands by, like a powerless spectator, to an enormous social and demographic event which has transformed their homeland and their society fundamentally.

As a contribution to a debate that has yet to take place, I submit the following views in the hope that when that debate does take place, diversity of views and opinions, will get the consideration they deserve. The time has come, in fact it's long overdue, to have that debate. The almost universally accepted view in the media, politics and the liberal elite, is that immigration is a positive development. A critical analysis of the evidence, if we can muster up the courage to look at it, might lead to the conclusion that this is anything but the case.

1

The Demographic Shift

For the last twenty years or more, a tectonic shift has been taking place in the demographic make-up of Western Europe. Ireland has been sleepwalking at the leading edge of this transformation. Tectonic shifts in the geological sense are imperceptible, until the point is reached at which the tension and pressure reaches gargantuan proportions. Suddenly the earth's surface ruptures and an enormous amount of pent up energy is released, usually with catastrophic consequences.

While this demographic transformation was blatantly obvious to the ordinary citizen, it did not seem to register at all on the political seismograph here in Ireland, or for that matter in Europe, until recently. If it had and the political will was there, remedial action could have been taken. But the elephant in the room is always disregarded until the house begins to fall down. Throughout the period and up to the present time, the patently obvious signs of this momentous change were ignored and pressure continued to build.

For Ireland, the principal source of the pressure at the beginning of this period, were the ten EU applicant states in Eastern Europe and their desire to access the EU labour market. Today and into the future, for Europe and Ireland, that demographic pressure is being generated by the widespread economic and social malaise in the poorer countries of Africa and Asia where structural, economic and cultural difficulties and a population explosion are being compounded by war and instability. The enormous problem of providing decent living standards for populations with very high growth rates is not easily solved, even in the best of circumstances. The less than benign conditions prevailing in Africa and parts of Asia today and into the foreseeable future, must inevitably lead to a prolonged period of migration. If jobs and livelihoods cannot be provided at home, those with the means will move. According to the United Nations, huge numbers of migrants are now on the move. Many of these people are likely to end up in Europe sooner or later. Unless substantial and rapid economic improvement takes place in their home countries, the number of migrants is likely to increase greatly in the coming years.

The good governance, sound institutions and respect for the rule of law that are believed to be a prerequisite for economic prosperity and social harmony, are absent or weak in many African and some Asian countries. The tribal and clan loyalties that permeate these societies can inhibit the trust that is required to create and sustain economic and social progress. This, together with very strong population growth, is at least part of the reason why they lag behind the rest of the world in economic development and why many of their people migrate. If this continues to be the case and there is every indication that it will, many more will attempt to move elsewhere and their destination of choice will be Europe.

In 1950, according to the UN, the total global population was 2.5 billion of which 225 million were Africans. In 2017 the global population was 7.55 billion of which 1.256 billion were Africans (a more than fivefold increase in sixty seven years). By 2100 the global population is projected to be 11.2 billion of which 4.47 billion will be Africans (an almost fourfold increase in the next eighty three years)[1]. That is an increase from 9 per cent of the world's population in 1950 to a whopping 40 per cent in 2100.

UN Population Projections (Report 2017)

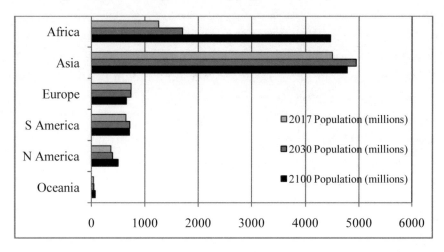

Fig. 1-1 The chart shows the UN world population projection in millions (UN World Population Prospects Report 2017) to the end of the century. It predicts that the world population will remain more or less stable apart from Africa where it will rocket – by 3.25 billion, almost quadrupling – in the next eighty years.

This UN projection, were it to prove true, would be an extraordinary global demographic upheaval by any stretch of the imagination. Four out of every ten people on the planet would be African or of African descent. If the present fairly loose migration policy in Europe is maintained, by the end of the century white Europeans could be a minority in Europe. Perhaps other large areas of the planet outside Africa would also have African majorities.

Looking at the African population explosion in more detail, the case of Nigeria illustrates the extent of the problem. The population of Nigeria in 1950 was 38 million, today (2018) it is

196 million and the UN projection for 2100 is a staggering 752 million, more than the entire population of the European Continent today, including Russia. In area terms, Nigeria is the size of the UK and France but by 2100 it will be six times more densely populated than these two countries are today − if Nigerians remain in their country − which, given the overcrowding factor, seems highly unlikely. With the Sahara Desert encroaching on West Africa, there could be serious environmental problems for Nigeria in the short to medium term, precipitating an even greater exodus of this huge population from the area.

Curiously, when the number one concern for the future of humanity − global warming − is discussed, the all-important link to over-population is seldom mentioned. The three-fold increase in the human population of the planet since 1950, which will become a five-fold increase by the end of this century − if we are unlucky, it could be a lot more − will have been contributed, almost exclusively, by the developing world. When economic development takes place, energy consumption surges and inevitably, so too do green-house gas emissions. With greater prosperity and increased consumption in the developing world, the pressure on the earth's already overstretched resources, will be enormous, as will the effects on the environment from the inevitable by-product of consumption − pollution. If these developments accelerate environmental deterioration even marginally, the likelihood is that they will also accelerate migration flows from these areas.

An important consideration in large scale movements of populations like we are seeing today, is that when people move, they bring their problems and attitudes with them. Few in the West would be happy to inherit the problems of Africa or the poorer parts of Asia. Apart from the cultural impediments of lack of trust, corruption and weak institutions outlined earlier, a number of other important factors may also contribute to an exodus from there and elsewhere in the future. The most important one, curiously, is that as the economies of poor countries grow, more people can afford to migrate. Improving health-care for children and the general population and disease control, while very welcome, will add significantly to population growth and in turn will increase pressure on resources. Environmental deterioration and overpopulation could be severe in vulnerable parts of Africa and indeed in the densely populated low lying areas of Asia. These factors and others, like instability and conflict are already leading to mass migration and as they intensify the levels of migration will undoubtedly rise.

This process is already well established. There is much evidence to show that rapid demographic change is happening all over Europe. In London, one of the great European cities, the native white British who formed 86 per cent of the inhabitants in 1971 were down to 45 per cent of the population in the 2011 census, making them a minority in their own capital city.

The New Plantation of Ireland

The Irish 2016 census figure (Central Statistics Office) for people residing here who were born outside Ireland – the UN defines a migrant as someone living in a country other than the one they were born in – is 810,406 people[2]. The UN figure for international migrants in Ireland in their 2017 Report is virtually the same at 807,000[3], or almost 17% of the population. Presumably, a small number of these would be children born to Irish parents living abroad, who had returned to Ireland. Since then (2016), the CSO has issued yearly 'Population and Migration Estimates', the latest one on the 27th August 2019[4] **(see Appendix 1)**. These estimates reveal that since the last census in 2016, a further net (arrivals minus departures) 93,900 non-national immigrants have arrived on our shores to live and work here, bringing the official total to 904,300 or 18.4% of the population. When the CSO speaks of non-nationals, it presumably excludes the 100,000+ group of non-Irish migrants who have been granted Irish citizenship and perhaps others. For my purposes, in examining the demographic shift in Ireland, I am comparing the indigenous Irish to all others, as one would if comparing native American Indians to the rest of the population of the United States or Canada.

These estimates also reveal some other fascinating facts. The CSO estimates that the growth in the population of Ireland in 2018 and in 2019 has been 64,500 in both years. The net non-national migrant influx in 2018 was 33,900 or 52.5% of that increase. The net non-national influx in 2019 was 35,800 or 55.5% of the increase in population of the country. This tells us that the non-Irish part of the population is increasing faster than the Irish part and that the rate of this increase is accelerating.

When we speak of demographic change, of course, this is not the whole story. The birth rate for non-Irish nationals is a huge component in the demographic transformation of Ireland. An article in The Irish Times on 20th November 2013 [5] relating to birth rates and migration said that 18% of births in Ireland in 2004 were to mothers from outside Ireland. That figure reached 25% in 2011 and was the same the following year. With the steadily increasing migrant population, it is probably safe to assume that the share of births of the children of migrants is also increasing. In the year to April 2019 the number of births in Ireland was 61,200 of which 15,300 were born to migrant mothers, if the 25% share of 2011 was maintained today.

Therefore, the increase in the population of Ireland (64,500) in the year to April 2019 was made up of 35,800 (net) newly arrived migrants, 15,300 new-born children of migrants and 45,900 indigenous Irish new-borns, making a total of 96,000 individuals. From that figure must be subtracted the 2,100 net indigenous Irish that left the country and the 30,400 deaths that occurred of overwhelmingly indigenous Irish. This brings the increase in the population of Ireland back to the CSO figure of 64,500.

This means the increase in the population of Ireland in the year to 2019 was 51,100 non-national migrants and the children of migrants, just short of 80% of the increase and 13,400 indigenous Irish children, the other indigenous Irish new-borns being cancelled out by indigenous deaths and emigration. This demographic transformation, by any standard, is a remarkable state of affairs. If this rate of change were maintained for a generation the indigenous Irish would be in the minority by 2050. We are, of course, already well on the way, with 900,000 adult migrants, anything between 200,000 to 300,000 children of migrants and an unknown number of undocumented, who don't feature at all in the official figures

These are the dynamics of the rapid demographic transformation taking place in Ireland today. A transformation that seems to have merited no discussion, no debate or no critical analysis. A transformation that has been hailed as a great 'progressive' step forward by the loudest voices in Irish society, in politics, business, the media and the liberal elite. A transformation so utterly fundamental, that it threatens to sweep away our unique identity, culture and traditions, which had survived a thousand years of colonial battering, invasions, expropriations and ethnic cleansings. A transformation that the English colonists of the sixteenth and seventeenth centuries tried but failed to achieve, despite their best efforts. A transformation in which we, the people of Ireland, have allowed a self-appointed authority to decree, that the public has no say in, whatsoever.

Perhaps this self-appointed authority is right. Perhaps none of this is important. Perhaps this is an inevitable consequence of the globalisation that the political and business elites have signed up to and that we have acquiesced in. Perhaps the populist insurgency in

Europe and the US that have challenged this transformation, is just a flash in the pan.

Ireland Leads the Charge in Demographic Change

While the people that set the agenda here are quite happy about the changes that are taking place and, to be fair, a large part of the population couldn't care, one way or the other and the rest have been effectively silenced, the transformation proceeds apace. Despite the devastating experience of the recent past, of hyper-expansion coupled with mass immigration, it has not even crossed the minds of successive Irish governments that this might not be a good thing, nor that they should do anything to curb the flow. In fact the reality is quite the opposite. Recently there have been numerous calls from employer organisations to increase the flow of inward migration. According to an article in *The Sunday Business Post* on the 6th January 2019 the American Chamber of Commerce (in Ireland) urged the Department of Business, Enterprise and Innovation to speed up work permit allocation to facilitate business[6]. This call was immediately responded to by the minister Heather Humphreys and echoed by her opposite number in Dail Eireann Billy Kelleher and the chief executive of the IDA (Industrial Development Authority), expressing regret for any delay and a contrite acknowledgement that the process was *'taking too long'*. It looked suspiciously like big business shouting jump and the government asking how high? To some neutral observers, this is a further confirmation of how Irish migration policy is being determined by big business. Now that the economy has improved, the flow of migrants has significantly increased and more than likely will accelerate, continuing the ethnic shift of the last twenty years away from the native population.

While Britain has been regarded as a multi-ethnic society since the 1950s, with 13.4 per cent of its present population being migrants (UN International Migration Report 2017), Ireland far surpasses that figure. We are leading the charge when it comes to rapid demographic change in Europe, far exceeding the UK, Germany, France, Denmark, Italy and Greece according to the UN(See Fig. 1-2 below). With net migrant annual influx numbers approaching 1 per cent of the population, we are again entering mass migration territory, where we could easily find ourselves in a minority in our own country sooner rather than later, as the ethnic British already have in London. The growth in the native Irish population from 2011 to 2016 (Census 2016 CSO) was just 0.8 per cent compared with a growth of 19 per cent for other nationalities in the Irish state.

These figures do not take into account undocumented migrants who may amount to a sizeable additional figure. The Migrant Rights Centre Ireland estimates that there are 20,000 to 26,000 undocumented people in the country (article in *The Irish Times*, 15 July 2017)[7] which seems very conservative when compared to Britain, where up to a third of recent arrivals are undocumented. Irish border controls are regarded as a laughingstock in some quarters, which is of course facilitating immigration fraud and illegal entry. A large number of asylum seekers arriving here, come from countries to which we have no transport links, indicating they have not registered in the country where they first reached safety (Dublin Convention), making their arrival here illegal.

With Ireland near the top of the league in Europe when it comes to the rate of demographic change, the story of how we got here does not reflect well on our ability to manage our own affairs or our borders.

Migrant percentage of the Population UN Report 2017

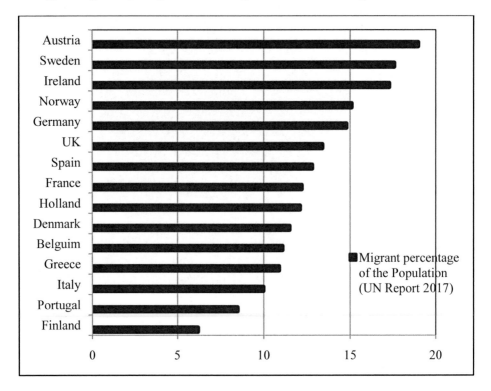

Fig. 1-2 The chart shows Ireland in third place among a leading group of countries to which migration takes place in Europe. Despite Ireland not being in the front line of recent migration surges, we still manage to have a higher migrant percentage of the population than Germany, the UK, Italy and Greece. (Source UN International Migration Report 2017: Highlights)

The Irish migration epic began in the early 1990s with the first stirrings of economic revival after a prolonged recession. The advent of the Celtic Tiger in the mid-1990s saw the beginnings of a large-scale influx of economic migrants into Ireland from Europe and Asia. They were mainly employed in low paid jobs in agriculture and food processing. Having developed a taste for cheap and flexible labour, Irish employers were soon employing migrants in many sectors of the economy. Between 2004 and 2008, following the accession of the ten new member states from Eastern Europe to the EU, a phase of intense inward migration took place into Ireland and to a lesser extent into the UK. The other members wisely refused access to their labour markets after 1st May 2004. This first experience of large-scale migration in recent times within the EU itself, was confined to Ireland and Britain and was not a major concern for Brussels.

Throughout the Celtic Tiger period the political establishment in Europe and the EU were preoccupied with other economic matters, the establishment of the euro on a firm footing and the Greek debt crisis. Navigating through these choppy economic waters it was guided by the four great articles of faith of the EU – freedom of movement of goods, capital, services and crucially, people. However, the UK, Ireland and Sweden were the only members to embrace the freedom of movement of people. This led to the prolonged episode of large-scale migration into Ireland that destabilised the Irish economy, leaving it vulnerable to the point of bankruptcy when the financial crisis struck in 2008.

For the EU, the free-for-all, light regulation policies of the Irish Government during the Celtic Tiger period were just a sideshow. We were 1 per cent of the EU economy and of little significance. The difficulties of the single currency and differences between the economic performances of the states in the euro-zone and the financial crisis of 2008 and its aftermath, were what concerned the EU Commission. Demographic change and cultural transformation were always secondary to trade and money making, if they were ever even considered. But this was soon to change.

Just over the horizon in North Africa and the Middle East the 'Arab Spring' had broken out in 2011 and with it a hoped for blossoming of democracy and peace. But before long, the factions and tribalism that had been repressed by autocratic rule reasserted themselves and the regions descended into bloodshed and mayhem. Libya, Egypt, Nigeria, Mali, Syria, Iraq, Afghanistan and Yemen all experienced war with varying levels of intensity. Large numbers of people were displaced and many made their way to the shores of the Mediterranean with a view to onward passage to Europe, safety and a better life. They were joining many others in a similar enterprise who were seeking to escape poverty and lack of opportunity in Africa and Asia. Demographic change and cultural transformation, already under way, were about to reach another level in Europe.

The Invitation

The long-standing turmoil in the Middle East that began with the Iranian Islamic revolution of 1979, had a destabilising effect on many Muslim countries and introduced the West to the concept of Jihad. Afghanistan has suffered conflict since before 1980, Iran and Iraq were at war for ten years in the 1980s and civil wars were ongoing or soon to start in Iraq, Syria, Afghanistan, Libya and Yemen. The more hopeful 'Arab Spring' of 2011 soon petered out, to be replaced by conflict which soon spread to North and West Africa. The situation had reached boiling point by 2014 and was manifesting itself on European borders in the form of record numbers of refugees and migrants seeking to gain entry to Europe.

By early 2015, with the Syrian conflict raging, the numbers had grown substantially and the increasingly desperate means they were prepared to take, drew extensive coverage in the media. The people trafficking operations across the Mediterranean and the Aegean were conducted with scant regard for safety and went almost unhindered by the authorities. A continuous stream of stories of drownings and exploitation and graphic images of suffering and distress disturbed and concerned public opinion in Europe.

The more practical and effective, but mundane efforts to help victims of the conflict in Syria, were happening behind the scenes in camps in Jordan, Lebanon and Turkey. This, however, played second fiddle to the drama at sea. Nevertheless, the hard lessons learned in Iraq, Afghanistan and Libya in the recent past, prevented any direct Western government involvement in Syria at the time, apart from some financial support for the refugee camps on the periphery of the conflict. Instead, remedial action was confined to Europe and the adjacent international waters of the Mediterranean.

By late summer 2015 the continuous media coverage had gradually built up a head of pressure for action on European leaders. Curiously, the rich Gulf States and Saudi Arabia offered no sanctuary to their Syrian fellow Muslims. On the contrary, they fanned the flames of sectarian hatred by assisting the numerous factions with weapons and war material.

Finally, after months of intense pressure in the media and from concerned humanitarian groups and others, the German Chancellor Angela Merkel issued that extraordinary open invitation to Syrian refugees to come to Germany in late August 2015.

The Guests Arrive

They did not need to be asked a second time. Within weeks 10,000 refugees and migrants a day were arriving in Germany and not just from Syria. On the weekend of 6 September 2015 in Munich alone, 6,800 arrived on trains, with 8,600 the following day and a further 2,200 that evening. They appeared to be mostly young men clutching the indispensable mobile phone. On the same weekend, it was reported that Greece's Migration Minister Iohannis Mouzalas rushed to Lesbos, the epicentre of the seaborne exodus, after riots and street battles broke out between migrants and local police. At one point 500 Afghans had attempted to seize a ferry bound for Athens.

By the end of 2015 almost one million people had arrived in Germany and more than 476,000 asylum applications had been made there. Frontex, the EU border agency put the total migration figure at 1.8million people entering Europe in 2015. It is difficult to say exactly who all these people were, as many of them destroyed their identity papers in transit. Probably about two fifths of those entering Germany were Syrians and most of the rest were Afghans, Iraqis, Kosovans, Albanians and North Africans.

In the first few weeks after the Merkel invitation, a feel-good atmosphere prevailed in Germany. There was a warm glow of pride, satisfaction and moral superiority, for having done the right thing, if reports in the media were to be believed. It was reminiscent of the euphoria that greeted the declaration of war in 1914. At that railway station in Munich on that first weekend in September 2015, the crowds clapped and cheered as the trainloads of migrants arrived. Merkel seemed to have read the popular mood perfectly.

Unfortunately, like all euphoric experiences, it didn't last long. As the numbers built up and facilities became stretched, anxiety began to set in. The German authorities soon realised that their unilateral decision to invite victims of the Syrian conflict had triggered a mass exodus from the Middle East and Africa as well[8]. It was time to play the European solidarity card.

Within two weeks of the enthusiastic welcome in Munich, EU interior ministers had met and decided that a quota system would be used to assign 120,000 refugees to other countries in the Schengen zone. Other EU members had a moral obligation to accept a proportion of the refugees. The new EU members in Eastern Europe were distinctly unenthusiastic. The Czech President Milos Zeman said *'only the future will show what a mistake this was'*. The Slovak prime minister refused to accept the decision.

While the implementation of the plan moved slowly, the migrant flow continued unabated. Their progress through Greece and the Balkans was unstoppable, as they overcame every obstacle on their way to Austria, Germany, Denmark and Sweden. National borders, their guards and police were overwhelmed. When transport was unavailable they walked. Borders, rules and bureaucracy were ignored in their single-minded march.

Europe was transfixed. Sympathy and pity was soon replaced, in some quarters at least, by fear and loathing. Even the most enthusiastic welcomers were having second thoughts. By December the Merkel mantra of 'we can manage' was wearing very thin. Germany was struggling to cope and resistance was growing in the native population at the prospect of permanently providing for a huge and growing population of migrants and refugees. By mid-March 2016 another 143,000 people had made the trip from Turkey to Greece.

In early 2016 a round of intense diplomatic activity between the EU and Turkey delivered a deal whereby the Turks would accept repatriated migrants from Greece, on condition the EU would resettle refugees from camps in Turkey. It also involved the payment of several billion euro to Turkey, visa-free access for their 75million mostly Muslim citizens to the EU and a speeding up of their application for membership of the EU.

Despite major clashes between the German and Turkish governments since, the migration deal is still in place and it seems to be working. The mass exodus from the Turkish mainland to the nearby Greek islands has all but ceased. This is a hopeful indication that with cooperation and concerted effort on behalf of the governments concerned, situations like this can be controlled. The focus of migration has now switched from the Aegean to the North African coast.

The Hangover

Thus ended, what may yet prove to be just another episode, in an ongoing continental mass migration situation. For Ireland, however, the large-scale migration phenomenon had begun much earlier with the birth of the Celtic Tiger in the mid-1990s. If anybody in Europe was interested, we in Ireland should have been able to tell them a thing or two about throwing open our doors and binging on the mass migration brew. But, on mature reflection, maybe that might not have been a good idea. We were never very good at critical analysis, learning from our mistakes or confronting painful realities.

In light of our reluctance to even mention, let alone discuss or analyse our own migration problems, would it have been wise to attempt to advise our neighbours on the pitfalls of the open door policy? What we could have told our European friends, was that we had an almighty hangover when the Celtic Tiger party ended in 2008 and despite the passage of time, it had not gone away.

We had a banking inquiry, we agonised about bond-holders and the property bubble but we failed to get to the root of the problem. The property splurge and the debt that financed it, the credit crunch and the bailout were all the result of attempting to accommodate a huge influx of migrants and in doing so, to make a financial killing. What the speculators and developers failed to anticipate, was the international financial crisis that overwhelmed the world economic system in 2008. The Irish financial institutions, in encouraging and facilitating the credit requirements of the property sector, had exposed themselves and more importantly, the Irish taxpayer, to an enormous amount of untenable risk. When the Crash came, the risk was realised, the debt was called in and the banks faced collapse. The reason why the banks took this extremely risky bet on property, was because they were convinced that the huge influx of migrants would continue unabated until at least 2020. When we attempted to analyse what went wrong in 2008, we continued to tiptoe around that elephant in the room. Like an embarrassing drunken episode, we could not bring ourselves to mention the 'M' word.

We have tried to put it to the back of our minds, but that massive hangover persists. To begin with, is the small matter of that €200 billion national debt. Where did we get all that money from and what did we do with it? Like Adam and Eve, in the EU Garden of Eden, a serpent in the form of a friendly European financial sector, with lots of spare cash looking for a good home, tempted us and we were seduced – well, some of us were. What we did with the money is not altogether clear.

Like the proverbial drunken sailor we spent it like water. We spent a lot of it on property, we spent a lot on doubtful government programmes, projects, quangos of all kinds and sweeteners we thought we could afford. Then, when the wheels came off the wagon, we spent the rest of it keeping the wolf from the door when our tax base collapsed and our social welfare bill went through the roof. Now we have to pay the piper.

We can comfort ourselves over the next couple of generations with the thought that bondholders, bankers and pensioners all over Europe and beyond will benefit by our foolishness. Meanwhile, as things improve, we are beginning to slip back into our old habits. When we changed governments – the recovery plan, the higher taxes and the reduced services – remained in place and our borders remained open. The government took cover behind the Troika for the most unpalatable bits. After an era of gross incompetence at the highest levels of government, the public service, business and banking, nobody was to blame. One individual went to jail, nobody lost their jobs – except for a few hundred thousand private sector workers. The architects of the debacle were just handsomely pensioned off while the taxpayer picked up the tab.

The economic cycle has now come full circle and we still have that infernal hangover. For good or bad, we have almost one million non-Irish residents in the state and undoubtedly many more to come. We have a serious housing crisis and it appears that even if houses were available, very few of us could afford them. We have a struggling health and education service and the previously mentioned €200 billion national debt, plus the €6 to 7 billion yearly interest bill that goes with it, among other things. Wages are rising moderately but taxation levels are high, leaving living standards for most working people more or less static. But, on the positive side, the business and property owning classes and our politicians have returned to the prosperity to which they had become accustomed. In recompense for having shouldered the burden, they have seen fit to reward the rest of us with a succession of socially 'progressive' referenda, which has made some of us feel a whole lot better, at very little cost.

The Great Recession which began in earnest in 2008 was a disaster for Ireland, Greece, Spain and Portugal. The other members of the EU endured a mild recession but were relatively unscathed. What made it worse for Ireland was mass immigration. Despite the damage and the disruption we suffered, we do not seem to have learned any lessons. We continue to allow levels of immigration into the country that (per capita) are way beyond what would be tolerated in Europe or even the United Kingdom. Not only are we putting up with it, but those of us who object are not allowed to question it. The one thing that has remained constant in an ever-changing Ireland is the flow of migrants into the country. It has been ramping up steadily in the aftermath of the crash. In 2014 the figure for non-Irish arrivals was 43,700 (CSO), in 2016 it was 54,100, and in 2018 it was 61,900.

The Guilt Trip

The repercussions in the UK of having high migration rates, half the Irish rates in per capita terms, were profound to say the very least. It was the most important factor in the British decision to leave the EU, which was probably the biggest political upset there since the Second World War. In Ireland, migration barely gets a mention in the media and is never seen as a problem. It does not feature on any political agenda but then again, neither did the madness and excess that accompanied the Celtic Tiger period. This will change sooner or later.

The effects of recent migration into other European countries, while not as radical as the UK decision to leave the EU, has also been politically very significant. The intense debate that has raged on the continent in the aftermath of the 2015 migrant crisis has shifted the political centre of gravity towards a more national-minded local agenda and away from individualism and globalisation. That debate has been sharpened by the spate of terrorist attacks inevitably linked to migration.

Ireland, with one of the highest levels of immigration in Europe over the last twenty years, has not yet joined the debate. Apart from the media consensus, on what amounts to censoring any robust or critical discussion on the issue and the strangle-hold of political correctness, that seems to have been adopted as a new theology by a large section of the population, there are other elements at work constraining our ability to confront this problem. Among them are our own apocalyptic experience of the Great Famine and its aftermath, that have never been fully rationalised or resolved and continue to inhibit our ability to think and act with maturity, leaving us prey to emotional blackmail. A residue of Catholic guilt about refusing the needy, may also be constraining the debate on migration. The host of NGOs, charities and other organisations, whose business it is to generate financial support for the poor of the developing world, by highlighting the difficulties of life there in contrast to our own relative prosperity, add more fuel to the guilt mountain. The cumulative effect of these and other factors plays a major role in inhibiting this vital discussion.

Apart from the appeal to our sympathy and solidarity as human beings, the approval of others, particularly our masters in Brussels who might not approve of ideas tinged with the heresy of populism, further constrains public discussion and critical analysis of the migration issue. Another inhibiting factor is the desire to appear sophisticated, cool and cosmopolitan, ready to embrace any number of seemingly exotic strangers. Haunted by the fear of appearing to be the primitive rednecks in the European out-back, we studiously avoid anything that might be construed as criticism of the migration orthodoxy.

The massive levels of emigration suffered by this country in the recent past, not to mention in the aftermath of the Great Famine, have scarred the national psyche and left us unable to think dispassionately about the issues surrounding our own immigration problem. Guilt – for still being here when so many had to leave – has combined with compassion to blind us to the disastrous consequences of allowing ourselves to be overwhelmed by a tsunami of migration, which threatens our identity, our culture, our institutions and our society. If we fail to call ourselves to order, if we do not curb our overgenerous instincts and get over our guilt, we will surely find ourselves in the same boat as our fellow Irishmen and women who did emigrate – not strangers in a foreign land, but in our own.

2

Political Correctness and the Liberal Consensus

All the talk of equality in Ireland today, is unfortunately, just that – talk. The civil rights issue of this generation was not the right to gay marriage identified by Eamon Gilmore of the Labour Party, but the fact that one half of the population, the bottom half – have been unceremoniously elbowed out of the way by a 'progressive' liberal elite. Important as gay marriage may be, and a majority have acknowledged that it is important, when compared to the creeping subversion of democracy, by a vocal, privileged group with a strong sense of mission, who make assumptions about what is good for the rest of us, then gay marriage slips down the list of priorities. Having hijacked the means of mass-communication and effectively gagged dissent, the 'progressive' elite has proceeded to implement a new moral, political and social order of political correctness on our behalf.

The capture of the commanding heights of our democracy by the liberal 'progressive' tendency has proved to be anything but progressive for many of us and near fatal for freedom of expression. It has stifled debate and strangled public discourse on the important issues of the day, which is essential to the proper functioning of a democracy. This self-appointed vanguard of a new enlightenment, have succeeded in enforcing an authoritarian 'liberal' ideology across the entire Irish political spectrum, with the result that a dense toxic pseudo-consensus has enveloped Irish public discourse.

This, of course, is not just an Irish phenomenon, it is a malaise of Western civilisation. The democratic deficit in the EU juggernaut, whereby the wishes of the people seem to be of little account in the great EU bureaucratic scheme of things, is reflected all over Europe. The forced march towards further and deeper integration by the EU Commission in the face of popular opposition, indicates scant regard for the people's concerns. The headline that has been set by the EU, from the start, of almost contemptuously brushing aside the tiresome concerns of the people, has been taken up with relish by the liberal establishments that still hold sway in most European capitals.

The emergence of the liberal elite as a dominant force, is in part at least, due to the atmosphere prevailing at our enormously expanded third level institutions. In 2016 we spent €3 billion more on education than our peers in Europe of a similar size, or almost one third more than the average. Some of that went into third level education to the benefit of the already better-off half of society. Despite the enormous resources consumed by these institutions, they are failing to produce the kind of graduates required for the Irish economy who must then be outsourced from other places. The Economic and Social Research Institute (ESRI) says Irish workers are the most overqualified in the EU for the jobs they have[1]. Over half of school leavers now attend university or third level of some kind, where the ethos is overwhelmingly liberal. Armed with the enlightenment of their liberal academic environment, their instincts and their votes naturally support that agenda. Their new found status as graduates, as every parent knows, inclines them to the belief that they know better than most.

The attitude born of this belief, has found a strong echo in the commentary following the Trump victory and the Brexit decision, where the defeated sides loudly bemoaned the lack of education and ignorance of the majority. The thinking behind this attitude appeared to be that democracy should be reserved for the clever and the educated – in the old days it used to be the property owning classes. The sense of entitlement of the Clinton supporters and the remainers in Britain was outraged by those shock defeats. They were so deeply offended that they could not accept the democratic wishes of the electorate and now seem hell bent on overturning the results by hook or by crook. A dangerous erosion of respect for democracy has taken place with extremely negative implications for society, not by Trump supporters or the Brexiteers but by the liberal progressive tendency.

The Liberal Elite

Their Irish equivalent is a growing new graduate class, an extended version of the upper middle-class, the well to do. They dominate business, the professions, the civil service, politics, the media and of course, education. They have most of the best jobs and they are used to getting their way. As the product of our universities, they are schooled in the progressive ideas of our time and immersed in the liberal atmosphere of the campus. They have broken free of the shackles of family life, place, tradition and religion and have encountered new people, new ideas and new nationalities. They feel the world is their oyster.

No wonder their counterparts in the United States and Britain were upset and annoyed at having their applecart up scuttled by what they considered to be an unruly ignorant mob. Ordinary people are fine, until they start getting ideas of their own. They are great for paying the taxes that fund our universities, building roads and houses and farming land, but let them stick to what they know best.

A great rift is now beginning to open up between the 'educated' and the rest in Western societies. This was always the case to some extent but the Trump and Brexit victories have brought the magnitude of the division into sharp relief and not just in the United Kingdom and the United States. The barely concealed contempt of Britain's remainers for Brexiteers and Clinton's supporters in America for what she called the 'deplorables', is a new fault line emerging in many societies, including Ireland.

The Victorians called them the 'great unwashed', Clinton called them the deplorables, they are the other half of society, the bottom half and they are slowly sinking and becoming economically and socially marginalised. They are the half that do not have university degrees. They are the low information voters who voted the wrong way. They used to be the middle-ranking working-class but their services are no longer required and now they are becoming the outsiders. They are the half of society whose wishes and concerns do not merit, or get, a hearing.

On the other hand, the new graduate class are the enlightened, the masters of the universe. They are the insiders, calling the shots in politics, economics and society. Their voice is always heard. Their guiding philosophy is 'progressive' individualism and is closely linked to ideas of the political correctness school of thought. The leading edge of 'the enlightened' have a very strong presence in the media, in politics and in education, which they use as a platform for disseminating their 'progressive' ideas. These include their own strident versions of gay rights, women's rights, immigrant rights, multiculturalism, globalism, environmentalism and equality of all kinds, except, crucially, economic equality.

The One Party State

The social agendas of all the political parties in the Irish state strongly reflect the concerns of the enlightened and the herd mentality, much in evidence in Dail Eireann, facilitates this. From the ragged tea-shirt to the smart suit, there are very few exceptions to the 'progressive' liberal agenda. Apart from a small group on the far left, there is also a general consensus on economic matters, with almost all politicians supporting free-market capitalism. This leaves the Irish voter with very little choice when it comes to political diversity. The only agenda on offer is the political platform of the enlightened, the progressive liberal individualist ideology. To all intents and purposes, Irish politics could be accommodated in a single 'Liberal Party'. The policy differences between most parties are an illusion, fostered in the interests of creating a separate identity for electoral purposes. Effectively, we live in a one party state.

Not that there is any lack of problems and issues confronting Irish society. What is lacking is diversity of ideas and the courage and vision to break free from the stifling 'progressive' consensus that rules the roost today. If members of Dail Eireann are to regain the respect of the people, they must stop looking over their shoulders for the approval of the ayatollahs of political correctness and get on with the job of managing the affairs of the country. There is no point in spending their time engaging in elaborate hair-splitting rituals when, in the end, the result is exactly the same. Today the two main political parties − who have been at each other's throats since the foundation of the state, in a Punch and Judy like farce, have little or nothing between them ideologically. The other smaller parties seem to spend their time virtue signalling on the side-lines, in a contest about who is the most 'progressive'. They all appear to have precisely the same position on company taxation, the EU, the environment, as well as most social and economic policy.

There is no such unanimity among the population. Contrary to the impression that might be gleaned from media commentary, 38 per cent of those who voted − 734,000 people − were against the gay-marriage proposition in the recent referendum. Despite this it was difficult to find a single politician to articulate their views. Effectively, more than one third of voters were politically voiceless. Only two TDs dared to put their head above the parapet and indicate their opposition. The conclusion to be drawn, is that a fundamental disconnect has opened up between politicians and people. Parliament no longer represents the views of all the people. Its members seem more interested in being on the winning side. Not only was robust political debate absent, but there was difficulty in finding opposing voices to articulate that view in the media and those who did, were treated with hostility, if not contempt. This has happened time and again in recent referenda and has now established a worrying and predictable pattern.

The most recent referendum on abortion is a further confirmation of the extent to which the 'One Party State' has become a reality in Ireland. Larissa Nolan, a media insider with strong liberal views, writing in the *Sunday Times* 27th May 2018 [(2)] makes the comment that on identifying as 'pro-life' in an industry (print media) that is evidently overwhelmingly pro-repeal *'I am a pariah, a heretic − I am the enemy'*. She later says that *'the entire political class, establishment and media are against your view'* (if you are pro-life). Welcome to the same alienation that half the population feel on a whole range of issues, stifled by the 'liberalism' that tolerates no diversity, the consensus that brooks no dissent. This is the intellectual straightjacket of the one-party State.

Dictatorship of the Commentariat

The liberal consensus in Dail Eireann is enforced by a self-appointed progressive politburo of individuals and organisations with strong politically correct views, no tolerance for diversity of opinion and ready access to the media. Their modus operandi is a pincer movement of the morally outraged mob on the one hand and the pathetic heart melting victim on the other. Both arms of the pincer are based on strong emotions, often to the exclusion of reason and common sense. This strategy has been used over and over again in the last couple of decades to guide public policy in the politically correct direction and at the same time, prise open the public purse. A whole industry has grown up around it, with a host of quangos, NGOs and charities all sucking on state finances, whether the taxpayer agrees with their agenda or not.

The progressive politburo, does not tolerate any form of what they decide to be, 'intolerance'. Those they deem to oppose tolerance and light, like Trump, Brexit, the Catholic Church, social conservatives, nationalists and pro-lifers, have made an implacable enemy and must be attacked and excoriated at every opportunity. Their enforcers are ever watchful for the heretic and the apostate. Over the last couple of years they have silenced at least two of the most prominent journalists in Ireland, John Waters and Kevin Myers who have dared to articulate alternative views. McCarthyism – with a twist – is alive and well in Ireland today.

The inevitable hue and cry that greets any divergence from the liberal agenda ensures that no discussion takes place on the subject of the Irish encounter with mass migration, in Dail Eireann or in any public forum. This subject is totally forbidden. Anyone who raises it will be branded a racist, a xenophobe, or a fascist and will be dealt with appropriately. They will be devoured by the progressive wolf packs that patrol the social media landscape. The authority to which we have entrusted the task of setting the boundaries of permissible views, has decreed this subject taboo.

The previous holder of the office of supreme moral authority, the Catholic Church, has now become the bête noir of the new regime. A convenient whipping boy is always useful in establishing one's credentials in these situations, especially one that is unlikely to bite back. Attacks on the Catholic Church have become a cost-free staple of Irish journalism for the last twenty-five years, unlike attacks on Islam or Judaism which could put life, limb or career in jeopardy. The acres of newsprint and untold volumes of broadcast hot air that have been expended in obsessing about the sins of the Catholic Church will, in time, become a fitting monument to the fearless and courageous nature of Irish journalism in the early twenty-first century. Ignoring the bastions of embedded privilege, lauding a motley crew of 'celebrities', defending tax-evasion – in the national interest of course – and promoting the latest fads in social engineering are the stock in trade of the Irish media.

While the guardians of virtue persist in throwing warlike shapes at the hobgoblins in the Catholic Church, the progressive tendency continues the important task of evangelisation in our schools and colleges. In common with the rest of the Western world, our third level institutions are the source of enlightenment for the new world order. Liberation from social, sexual, religious, cultural and national constraints is the objective. From the ivory towers of academia, the benign light of political correctness permeates every corner of society. It believes passionately in democracy, but only when it is liberal, when the people deliver the 'right' answer. It abhors populism, the democracy of the sweaty, uneducated lower orders.

The solution to the difficulty of ignorant people with primitive ideas having the vote, as has happened with Brexit and Trump, is there in plain sight. Democracy, if it were arranged like the Seanad Eireann election, where only graduates could vote, could probably be depended upon to deliver the right answers. Luckily, for the rest of us, for the moment at least, this is not the case. People, regardless of their educational status still have a vote. But there is more than one way to skin a cat, and as insiders, the progressive tendency is not above manipulating events and circumstances in the service of their own objectives. The clearly expressed will of the majority is always vulnerable to the wiles and strategies of a determined opponent with the inside track, as we saw in Britain recently.

However, the will of the people can only be frustrated for so long. There is no doubt that the populist insurgency has greatly unsettled the establishment in the West. The initial shock and horror has been replaced by a scramble to appear to accommodate the concerns of people who were ignored up to now. The liberal establishment will use every ploy and device to outmanoeuvre the populist movement and hold on to power, but it may already be too late. The populist revolt has spread throughout the West and has made a significant impact on politics in Europe and the United States. The liberal consensus that served the elite so well is about to be challenged.

Crisis of Identity for the Left

The first victim of the challenge to the old order is the concept of the political spectrum, with its right wing conservatism and left wing socialism. This spectrum, as a political yardstick, is rapidly becoming redundant. The second victim may well be left wing politics itself. In a complete reversal, it appears that the left, once the voice of the working class has become the voice of the privileged and the right has become the voice of the workers. The Trump victory in America is a spectacular illustration of this phenomenon. The working people of America turned their back on the Democratic Party, once the champion of the working class and supported Trump the arch capitalist. They supported Trump, not because they were taken by his personality or believed in his half-baked ideas but because he articulated, at least some of their concerns. The Democratic candidate, who characterised the Trump supporters as 'deplorables', was backed by a well-educated urban middle-class, a cohort of libertarian interest groups and minorities and almost the entire media.

Another manifestation of the crumbling of the old political ideologies of right and left was the Brexit vote. British working people turned their backs on the Labour Party who had called for a 'remain' vote and had failed to articulate their concerns on immigration. It was the UK Independence Party (UKIP) and a section of the Conservatives who forced the referendum that let the people speak, not the champions of the working class. It was the right that heard the roar. Again, it was the educated middle-class, minority interest groups and the liberal 'progressive' media, who opposed it. The British Labour Party had long been in decline. It is now in the process of abandoning the working-class in favour of the new graduate class, which has led to a partial revival in its fortunes. Its membership is now around 60 per cent graduates.

There is a fundamental crisis of identity in left wing politics all over Europe and here in Ireland. A shrinking working-class and a growing under-class are deserting the left and moving to the populist parties. The left today appears to be in the process of transforming itself into another manifestation of liberal politics. In this, it is in competition with most other political parties. It is no longer interested in economic inequality, which was always a hard nut to crack. It now busies itself with the more fashionable and less resistant issues of environmentalism, gender politics, women's rights and the general concerns of the middle class. A classic example of this was the grandiose claim made by Eamon Gilmore, referred to earlier, that gay marriage was 'the civil rights issue of this generation'. Voters recognised this bandwagon hijack for what it was and soon let their feelings about the Labour Party priorities be known at the February 2016 general election.

Left wing politics, in its drift into liberalism, has abandoned the economic advancement of the bottom half of society. The clearest and most emphatic evidence for this is its stance on immigration. The left has chosen to stand with liberalism and fashionable politics, on this fundamental issue for working people and the indigenous poor. The advent of large-scale migration creates a glut in the labour market. In a free market economy it inevitably means that the price of labour falls, in the same way as the price of commodities fall in a situation of oversupply. Labour dumping forces wages down. This is how markets work. Particularly affected are those at the lower end of the labour market, where most of the newly-arrived migrants are concentrated. Migration does not affect the stockbroker or the lawyer.

As the priorities of the Left change, from defending the economic interests of native working people to championing the causes of the middle-class, including the interests of minorities with whom workers are in competition, so a dispute arises. Workers can hardly be expected to support those who support the competition. This process of disengagement is currently in progress and may, if it continues, totally alienate the bottom half of society from left wing politics.

Some of the citizens of Europe have been offered a real choice in elections recently, for the first time in decades. Not between right and left, but between libertarian, global, individualism championed by the progressive left on the one hand and country, community, culture, identity and family championed by the populist parties. The traditional left prioritised the group over the individual, the many over the few, the poor over the rich. Today the left espouses the merits of liberalism, which is essentially about the freedom of the individual to pursue his or her own agenda regardless of others, economically and socially, the polar opposite of the traditional left.

The handmaiden of liberalism is globalisation. In the globalised scenario the confining nature of national borders, culture and tradition are dispensed with and the individual is at liberty to pursue his or her own agenda wherever he or she likes, regardless of local objections. He is a citizen of the world, a free agent, in a borderless world. The legal framework required to support him in the pursuit of his agenda, is an integral part of globalisation. The EU is globalization in microcosm. Laws, rules and institutions are constructed at Commission level by an army of well-paid technocrats – not by Parliament – and countries or communities have very little say in the outcomes. In the fully globalised scenario they will have even less.

The free movement of capital is an inherent part of globalisation, with all its economic and indeed social implications. The World Bank and the International Monetary Fund are global institutions that often dictate and enforce economic policy in many countries, in the interests of international capital and the underlying globalisation agenda. Their activities are portrayed as restoring economic order, when in fact they are often the enforcers for the local extractive elites and multinational corporations. Their interventions, dressed up as treatment for ailing economies, often have devastating social and economic consequences for the poor and vulnerable in these countries. In espousing the merits of liberalism the left is also embracing globalisation with all its often negative implications for the less well-off.

Social Partnership

In Ireland, the transition from communitarianism to liberalism has been taking place on the left for the last twenty five years. While the left struggled with its conscience, the trade union movement set about the practical business of climbing on board the Celtic Tiger bandwagon, in exchange for co-operation and flexibility on behalf of its members.

An important element in the creation of the Celtic Tiger was the social partnership model of co-operation between government, business and labour (represented by the Irish Congress of Trade Unions). From 1987 until 2008, a series of agreements between the partners ensured stability, peaceful industrial relations, moderate wage increases and progress on some socio-economic issues. This benign climate fostered the rapid economic growth in the Celtic Tiger years, at minimal cost to the business sector. By getting agreement to fix labour costs, business was able to keep most of the wealth generated by the phenomenal growth that took place here, which was the envy of every developed country.

An all-enveloping consensus emerged in politics, business and the trade-unions, in the 1980s which lasted until the crash in 2008. The rapid economic growth, buoyant taxes, fixed labour costs and some moderate gains for workers, all combined to reinforce that consensus. Business was booming. Taxes poured into the exchequer, to the extent that we could even afford a rainy day fund. It was only when it all fell apart after the crash, that the strength and sustainability of the economy were questioned. Mary Harney admitted as much when she said at the Banking Inquiry, that government should be *'more questioning, particularly of consensus'*.

Social partnership was consensus made flesh – the practical expression of the concept. It was the toast of the captains of industry and no wonder. It had delivered workplace harmony, flexibility and productivity at a very reasonable cost. On the union side, it had secured what was considered – especially by government and employers – to be a reasonable deal for union members nationwide in just one negotiation, instead of having to strike a deal on every site, with all the hassle, time and conflict that process would entail. It had of course the inevitable drawbacks of a one-size-fits-all deal, which meant that weaker groups and non-unionised workers piggybacked on the strength of the well organised. The unions, in accepting the social partnership concept, were conceding the advantages of an individualised market-type approach, where unionised employments could wring a better deal out of employers. The collective approach – a contradiction, in an individualised world – where partnership was delivering for business and government, was not only acceptable but laudable. In hindsight this was a huge mistake, in that it allowed business to reap the rewards of the Celtic Tiger boom unhindered, for a fixed labour cost that was on the low side. The worker share of the national wealth cake was shrinking under social partnership. It also allowed the economy to get out of control because the breaking mechanism of increasing wages was never applied. Market forces were allowed free reign for business and capital, while collective constraint applied to workers. When circumstances changed after the crash and it no longer suited their purposes, employers immediately abandoned the approach.

In the longer term, social partnership undermined the whole basis for the existence of the trade union movement. Why would anyone join a union when exactly the same terms and conditions could be had for free? The only thing on offer for the trade unions was that the union leadership got their feet under the top table, with the most powerful people in government and industry and enjoyed the illusion, as it turned out, that they were making big decisions with the big boys. Government, as the third party to the troika, were delighted with the ringing coffers at the revenue. The consensus was delivering - the message from the top table was that this was a win-win for everybody.

3

The Left Looses the Plot

Social partnership was delivering for business, government and to some extent for the Irish Congress of Trade Unions (ICTU) and its members, but it's always when things are going well that greed raises its ugly head. Plenty is never enough. Harmony, flexibility and productivity at a very reasonable cost, were not enough for some employers. The ocean of cheap labour out there beyond our shores was beckoning, just waiting to be exploited and they were determined to get their hands on it. In the 1990s the Irish employers' love affair with migrant labour began, and it continues undimmed to this day.

Immigration into Ireland began in earnest in 1996 when 21,500 non-nationals arrived. By 2000 the total of new arrivals in the previous five years had reached 116,600 or 3 per cent of the population and by the end of 2004 it was 273,500. The warning lights should have gone on in 2002 when it had reached, what the Germans and most other people came to consider mass migration levels. That year the arrival figure was over 40,000 or 1 per cent of the Irish population - the German per capita equivalent of the 2015 mass migration influx from Syria. By May 2004 it had racked up the staggering figure of almost 7 per cent of the population in nine years, even before unfettered access came into force. That indicated a rate of demographic, economic, cultural and social change, in a short period, way in excess of that experienced by any of our European neighbours including Britain. But at that stage, it was only the prelude, it was just getting started.

Such was the enthusiasm at official level for unrestricted migration that as early as the spring of 2002 the Irish Government had decided, without any discussion in Dail Eireann or consultation with the Irish people, to allow unfettered access to the citizens of the ten applicant countries for EU membership from Eastern Europe, to live and work in Ireland from the date of their acceptance as members.

An article in the *Sunday Business Post* in June 2002[1], which went almost unnoticed, revealed that the Irish Government had given an unsolicited commitment in writing to the governments of the applicant states to this effect, despite the fact that the other EU members had given no such commitment. Of the fifteen member states, only Ireland, Britain and Sweden granted unfettered access, while the rest wisely held back until the last minute and then invoked their right to restricted access – for the full seven years as it turned out – allowable under EU rules.

The Irish Business Employers Confederation (IBEC), unsurprisingly, was another unfettered access enthusiast. The prospect of an endless supply of cheap, well educated, pliant workers was a-dream-come-true for their members. Another sizable beneficial effect for employers was the dampening of the expectations of the domestic workforce, on foot of the competition created by the unlimited influx of cheap labour. These two factors were the key to the unprecedented prosperity of many businesses in the Celtic Tiger period. These were the arguments that contributed in no small way to persuading the government – always anxious to facilitate the business sector – to take the action they did, in opening up the Irish labour market to intense competition from Eastern Europe.

What was much more difficult to understand was the enthusiasm of the ICTU for unfettered access. While the traditional left, in their capacity as the representatives of the downtrodden, might have been tempted to embrace migration as the solution to the problems of the global poor, common sense and the experience of the past, should surely have indicated that this would contribute little to the resolution of the global problem and be more likely to worsen things at home. The business of the trade union movement, while related in a general way to the objectives of the left, should have had an altogether different set of priorities. The first duty of a trade union is to represent the interests of its membership. That is why members pay their subs. Nevertheless, while their peers in twelve of the fifteen EU states (at that time), objected to granting access to their labour markets, the ICTU acquiesced in a disastrous policy that accelerated immigration into Ireland, undermined the interests of their members and within a short period led to the near collapse of the economy.

The Alarm Bell Goes Off

I had been a trade union member, shop steward, Trades Council member and activist for the previous thirty years and was very familiar with the concerns of workers. Having observed with alarm the growing influx and the increasingly cavalier and reckless management style of government, banks and business, I wrote to the members of the ICTU Executive on 1st March 2004 expressing my concern and dismay at the prospect of unfettered access by the ten new member states. This was my letter:

1st March 2004

Dear ICTU Executive Member

It seems that Ireland is now the only EU state with an open-door policy on migration from the new states joining the EU in May. This is a disastrous policy as far as Irish workers and their families are concerned and I hope the Irish Congress of Trade Unions will seek, with all the pressure at its disposal, to have this policy reversed. This is probably a vain hope but nonetheless the argument must be made.

I am appalled at the lack of understanding by the ICTU of the issues that concern Irish workers to-day. While the share of wealth enjoyed by workers declines as a proportion of the overall wealth generated by them, the ICTU concerns itself with every fashionable pseudo-liberal cause of the day. It certainly gets first prize for the most politically correct organization in the country but if it were a company board it would be sacked long ago. The last thing on its mind is the interests of its paying members.

The other fourteen member states have wisely decided to restrict access to their economies for a considerable period while our Government, because it suits the desire of business for unlimited cheap labour, has persisted in the folly of the open door policy. The effect of this policy is equivalent to dumping on the labour market which in turn will depress wages across all sectors. Has the ICTU been in bed with the social partners for so long now that it does not realise that it is being put upon?

With a non-national population in excess of a quarter of a million at the moment the pressure on our infrastructure and prices is having a seriously detrimental effect on the lives of workers and their families and their quality of life. Market forces are allowed to push up prices but not the price of labour, because of the dumping referred to earlier. Our hospitals and schools cannot provide the services that people have paid for through their taxes and insurance contributions over the years. Young people can't afford to buy a house because speculators have crowded them out of the market. When our children enter the labour market they must compete for jobs at the minimum wage rate while the cost of living goes through the roof. The one hundred and seventy thousand unemployed will never get work again if unlimited access is granted to migrant labour. All these issues will be further compromised by the Governments open door to migrants.

The UN has estimated that there are currently two hundred and thirty million migrants worldwide. Many of these people are living lonely, exploited and miserable lives and would prefer to live at home if economic circumstances were better. It is up to business and Governments to encourage investment and job creation where plentiful supplies of labour are available thereby building up the economies of poorer countries. In Ireland our business and capital tax policies are robbing the developing world of investment they badly need. The ICTU has not uttered a word about this despite it being against ICTU policy. What's the point of creating two hundred jobs in Ireland and bringing in two hundred people – probably exploiting them, putting extra pressure on an overstretched infrastructure and getting a grant from the Irish taxpayer into the bargain?

Most of us who want to indulge our own pet projects, causes or beliefs do so at our own expense and in our own time. When we are engaged to carry out work at an employer's expense we concentrate on the job in hand or we don't get paid. The job that trade union members are paying for is the job of protecting the wages and conditions of the paying members. It is a difficult and demanding job that requires single-minded dedication to the interests of those who are paying for it.

Yours sincerely,

Frank Cosgrove

I got two replies, one from Jack O'Connor of SIPTU and the other from David Begg General Secretary of the ICTU. Mr O'Connor's reply was a bland reassurance that everything was under control. In fairness to Mr Begg, he did take the time and trouble to consider and reply to my letter. I believe the sentiments expressed were his sincerely held views. Unfortunately, for working people, many of his arguments were lacking in merit.

This was what he said: (2) **(See Appendix 2)**

5 April 2004

Dear Mr. Cosgrove,

Thank you for your letter which, despite its many insulting comments and derogatory tone, raises a few interesting points.

If allowing workers from the new member states access to Ireland turns out to be the "disastrous policy" you fear, it is open to the Government to change that policy. There is no evidence to show that current policy will result in migrant workers flooding the Irish labour market. It is also very important to appreciate the substantial contribution migrant workers have already made to our economy and society. We will continue to need this contribution in the future.

On the specific issue of labour substitution, Congress and our affiliated unions have been involved in lengthy discussions with the Department of Enterprise, Trade and Employment to agree policies and procedures aimed at protecting the jobs of Irish workers. We believe it is possible to do this without locking out workers from other EU countries. Irish workers and Irish society have benefited greatly from having access to other countries in the past and continue to do so.

We are well aware of the pressures on the lives of working people and their families caused by the lack of adequate housing, hospitals, schools and other infrastructures. Congress is involved in intensive negotiating and lobbying to have our social services and general infrastructure improved and developed. Our efforts in this important area have met with varying degrees of success. For example, the initiative on affordable housing which we negotiated as part of Sustaining Progress should deliver a home for ten thousand young couples.

You rightly state the job that trade union members are paying us for is "protecting wages and conditions". The wage increases which we negotiate are voted on by union members in democratic ballots. It is the members who decide whether the increases are adequate. Protecting the value of wage increases involves dealing with other issues like taxation and inflation while protecting conditions involves a wide range of provisions from pensions and holidays to child care and healthy work environments.

As far as your complaint about 'pet projects' is concerned, campaigning for equality for all workers, irrespective of nationality, is not some optional 'add on' for Congress. It is spelled out very clearly in our constitution under OBJECTS OF CONGRESS parg. (b): "To ensure full equality in all aspects of employment opportunity and to oppose discrimination on any such grounds as colour, ethnic or national origins, politics, race, religion, sex, age and disability."

Congress will continue to oppose discrimination and fight for equal employment opportunities for all workers while remaining vigilant to the danger of some employers using 'foreign' workers as cheap labour to displace indigenous workers.

Yours sincerely

David Begg   GENERAL SECRETARY

This was an important letter, because of the light it shed on the attitude of the leadership of the trade union movement, at the highest level, to a key issue. At the point when, as a member of the social partnership setup, the ICTU could and should have insisted on the government retaining control of, and access to our labour market, in line with almost all of our peers in Europe, it failed utterly. The ICTU failed the trade union movement and the membership and in doing so it exposed Irish workers to an unprecedented level of labour dumping. It is no exaggeration to say that this has adversely affected the living standards, wages and job security of a whole generation of working people. It also exposed the Irish economy to a wholly unsustainable level of inward migration that almost bankrupted the country, undermined the structures of our welfare state and eroded the delicate dynamics of social cohesion. While it may have been an unintentional misjudgement, stumbled into on foot of the cosy consensus of social partnership, the consequences of unfettered access have been catastrophic for Irish workers and their families, in terms of lower incomes, higher taxes, stretched educational and health services and a property bubble.

The ICTU Blunder

It is apparent from the letter that no effort whatsoever was made to modify government policy in relation to access. It is, or should be the business of the ICTU, to lobby the Government with regard to policies which would affect their members in the first place and workers in general. Obviously, IBEC very effectively lobbied the government to do something which was completely out of line with our peers and which the other twelve EU members would not do, which was to grant unfettered access. Did it even cross the minds of the ICTU that this might be a bad idea? Did anyone in the ICTU examine the reasons why the other member states and their worker representatives refused access?

Mr Begg's letter states *'There is no evidence'* to show that *'migrant workers will flood the Irish labour market'*. In the three years before accession (of the ten new members) and this letter, 800 people a week were arriving in Ireland to take up residence and employment here. If that is not evidence of a flood then what is? In 2003 the inward migration rate for non-nationals was running at 42,400 a year. This is the German per capita equivalent of 800,000 people a year, a little less than the migrant crisis figure for 2015. It all depends on what one considers a flood of course, one man's flood being a mere puddle in some trade union circles. Certainly the majority of Germans in 2015 considered a similar sized influx, a flood. For most people back in 2004, this should have been solid evidence that caution was required.

Mr Begg in the opening part of his letter (paragraph 2) states that *'it is open to the Government to change that policy'* if it turns out to be disastrous. Imagine telling Irish farmers that the government is going to allow free access to beef and dairy products from anywhere in the world. The farmers would not wait to find out if it was a disaster – they would know a disaster when they saw one. Most people try to take preventative action before a disaster happens. As a social partner, the ICTU should have resisted this policy from the time it was first mooted, studied the evidence and built a case to stop it, as its European peers had successfully done. If the policy had nonetheless been implemented, it should have renewed the attack after its first year in operation, when it became patently obvious that in fact the labour market was being flooded. In 2005, the first full year after enlargement, non-national inward migration rocketed from 41,800 to 66,000 (CSO). The 2005 figure is the German equivalent of almost 1.25 million people.

At the end of the paragraph he acknowledged the substantial contribution migrant workers had made. This may well have been true, but at the time that Mr Begg wrote his letter there were 171,000 people on the dole, many of whom could have been trained to fill whatever vacancies were available and whose welfare should have been upper-most in the mind of the ICTU. God knows, we were spending enough money on FAS (the national training agency) at the time. That approach would also have had the beneficial effect of reducing Social Welfare expenditure for the taxpayer.

In the third paragraph of the letter he dealt with the issue of 'labour substitution'. We are told congress had agreed policies and procedures with the Department of Enterprise, Trade and Employment to protect the jobs of Irish workers. This sounded distinctly like a cloud of hot air. And that is exactly what it proved to be. This claim was comprehensively debunked within eighteen months, when, in the autumn of 2005 Irish Ferries sacked their Irish workforce and replaced the 543 workers with cheaper foreign labour, according to an article in the *Irish Independent* 26 November 2005 [3] **(see Appendix 3)**. Even at that stage there was still time to call a halt to the unfettered access fiasco, but congress again failed to act.

Stop Labour Dumping

The Taoiseach Bertie Ahern is quoted in the same article by Senan Maloney (in the *Irish Independent* 26 November 2005) in regard to the Irish Ferries row, saying that 'nothing could be done'. So much for the policies and procedures agreed with the Department of Enterprise, Trade and Employment. The deadline for re-imposing restrictions on access by the ten new member states was 30th April 2006 and instead of relying on worthless 'policies and procedures', this was the time for congress to insist on restrictions or withdraw from social partnership.

Instead, congress embarked on a futile and utterly useless campaign of protest. Jack O'Connor the SIPTU boss is quoted in the *Irish Independent* on 31st October 2005[4] as warning that the proposed Services Directive in Europe would allow companies to bring cheap workers across from the continent. There was no need for companies to bring them in – they were here already. Mr O'Connor warned of a neo-liberal nightmare, which was just more useless hand wringing. He did not call for the only effective response which was the re-imposition of restricted access to our labour market, while there was still time, like our neighbours in Europe were implementing.

This fundamental blunder by the trade union leadership had and will continue to have enormous negative consequences for Irish workers for the foreseeable future, in terms of displacement, unemployment, lower wages and higher taxation. While it might not have been possible to convince the government to revoke the unfettered access, the ICTU appear to have failed to even raise the issue.

The labour substitution row in the Autumn of 2005 exposed the full extent to which the Irish Trade Union movement had become a captive of Political Correctness ideology. It's commitment to the equality of all workers – newly arrived migrants or ununionized (as articulated in Mr. Begg's letter) – played straight into the hands of the cheap labour lobby. It constrained its defence of the interests of its Irish paying members and undermined the market for their labour. It displayed a remarkable level of naivety.

The extent of the Political Correctness takeover was illustrated by a minor incident that took place at the time. I attended a protest march in Dublin on 9 December 2005, in relation to the Irish Ferries row. When I reached the Garden of Remembrance, I unveiled my placard which read 'STOP LABOUR DUMPING'. I wasn't surprised, when almost immediately, I was confronted by a steward who told me that I would not be allowed to display the placard, presumably because it was the last thing the ICTU was prepared to do. I protested and despite the hostility, I did take part in the march with the placard displayed.

When David Begg says that the efforts of congress 'have met with varying levels of success' on the broader economic front, he is making a greatly exaggerated claim. Congress in 2004 presided over a workforce whose efforts were generating enormous wealth, while they were earning a shrinking slice of the national wealth cake. This was acknowledged as far back as autumn 2000 by the Economic and Social Research Institute (ESRI) in an article in the *Irish Independent* 15 September 2000[5] where it said *'workers were getting a smaller slice of the national cake, with more going to make up huge corporate profits and higher rents'*. The partnership agreements delivered modest increases in return for increased productivity and flexibility. Real earnings growth for workers in the 1990s was 1.7 per cent, in the 2000s it was 1.4 per cent, and in the 2010s to 2015 it was just 0.6 per cent, mostly under partnership agreements – modest indeed. Meanwhile the economy grew at a phenomenal yearly average of 10 per cent between 1995 and 2000 and at 5.5 per cent from 2001 to 2007. This was a bad deal for workers in terms of wages and salaries versus productivity delivered and the main reason why business got away with it was that the labour market was in oversupply due to immigration.

At the same time house price inflation took off, panicking many working people into paying inflated prices that would soon trap them in negative equity. As to the claim that congress had negotiated 10,000 affordable houses in 2004, only 3,539 local authority houses and 1,607 voluntary and co-operative houses were built. This was barely enough to accommodate one fifth of the 66,000 migrants that had arrived that year, most of whom were penniless. As David Begg says in his letter, congress were rightly concerned at the lack of hospitals, schools and other infrastructure, but the one thing they could have done to mitigate these circumstances they failed to do, which was to object to the massive numbers pouring into the country, who, once they were here, were using all these services.

On the question of the duties of unions and congress to union members, Mr Begg acknowledges that the job trade union members are paying their unions for is to protect their wages and conditions. In their capacity as paying members, they are part of an exclusive club that pays for a service. Exclusivity, by definition, implies that others are excluded, in this case those that do not pay– just like your local golf club. Trade unions and congress should concern themselves with the interests of those who pay, as their top priority. If they concern themselves with everybody's problems, then what is the point of being a trade union member? Is it any wonder that trade union membership has been falling steadily for the past fifteen years, now representing only about 25 per cent of the workforce? The participation of congress and the trade union movement in social partnership after 2004, actively encouraged and supported policies that led to mass immigration and the inevitable labour dumping that accompanied it and was against the interests of union members and indigenous workers in general.

Equality?

Labour organisations and governments on the continent rightly anticipated a large influx of migrants from the new member states in 2004 and had no qualms about excluding them and thereby protecting their labour markets. We should have followed their lead. Mr Begg's letter, in the closing paragraphs, indicates that the Irish trade union movement had firmly nailed its colours to the mast of political correctness, regardless of the effects on 'indigenous' workers and their own members. The new watchword was 'equality', whether you had worked here for thirty years or had just stepped off the plane from Poland. You were equal, whether or not you had paid your union dues.

When Gordon Brown uttered those infamous words at the British Labour Party conference in 2007, *'British jobs for British workers'* he was speaking for the majority of British workers. It was just a pity he didn't mean what he said. British workers have not changed their minds, unlike Mr. Brown. That was why they voted for Brexit in 2016. Three years before the Gordon Brown utterance our own David Begg, on behalf of the Irish trade union movement, rejected any notion that Irish people should have any prior right to Irish jobs. The idea of national preference for Irish people in Ireland was, according to the ICTU, 'discriminatory'.

Not only that, but in his letter to me in regard to unfettered access, Mr Begg pledged congress to campaign for equality for all workers, irrespective of nationality and the other usual laudable grounds. The necessarily exclusive or even discriminatory privileges of trade union membership enjoyed by members, by virtue of their paid-up status, apparently was irrelevant in the eyes of the Irish Congress of Trade Unions.

Equality, of course, is a widely held idea and a founding tenet of 'progressive' liberal philosophy. The principle of 'equality for all workers, irrespective of nationality' is on the face of it, a laudable aspiration, but effectively it reduces the value of nationality to zero, which, from the liberal point of view is no bad thing. Unfortunately, in the mass immigration scenario, the equality it delivers is the depressed wage rates of a labour market in oversupply. As we all should know, the market does not respond to high-minded aspirations. The market, whether it is oil, land, lead or labour, responds to two implacable laws − supply and demand. There are many examples of this inexorable process at work. We need look no further than the United Kingdom, the United States and indeed ourselves, to see that the overall effect of large scale immigration is effectively income stagnation for workers in these countries. This has been the case in Ireland since the 2008 crash and for a much longer period in some economies.

In a fully globalised world with free movement of labour, the globalised labour market would pit the one billion people of the developed world against the six and a half billion of the developing world. The effect would be a collapse in income and living standards for workers in the developed world, as their wages plummet to meet the much lower levels of their peers in the less fortunate developing world. By such means would that laudable aspiration, 'equality for all workers, irrespective of nationality' be achieved.

What seems to be happening at the moment is that this very scenario is playing out in slow motion. Stagnating living standards for working people has been a feature of Western economies since well before the turn of the century. The transfer of industrial production to low cost economies where labour is dirt cheap, leaving rust belts and large numbers of unemployed manual workers, is part of this process. When large-scale inward immigration is added to this scenario the downward pressure on labour markets increases even further. This is what the cheerleaders for globalisation at Davos and such gatherings have to offer workers in the developed world. As the globalisation band wagon proceeds, some very painful side effects may well emerge and not just for working people. The pre-eminent position of the upper middle class may also come under increasing pressure from outside competition, technological developments and migration. If and when this happens support for the liberal consensus may well begin to evaporate.

For the trade union movement, the writing seems to be on the wall. A serious, steady, if not fatal shrinkage in membership is taking place. The heady days of the Celtic Tiger, when social partnership created the illusion that workers had a seat at the top table and could influence important events are long gone. The monumental blunder of allowing a tsunami of migration to swamp our economy, while not directly attributable to the trade union movement has, by association, gravely wounded it. The loss of confidence in its judgement and leadership and its failure of courage to challenge a toxic consensus, may further hasten its decline.

The Open Door and the Big Lie

Numerous EU studies, journalists, politicians, stock-brokers and the ICTU, all assured us that everything would be fine and that a flood of migrants would not arrive here. Was this wishful thinking, naivety, or plain stupidity, or was it an underlying feeling that a large dose of migration would be good for our mono-cultural malaise? Whatever it was, in 2004, the year of accession of ten new member states from Eastern Europe, the flood of migrants from the east suddenly became a tsunami. The print media seemed to be in denial about the situation. Willy Dillon's article in the *Irish Independent* on 14th February 2004[(6)] stated *'There are a little over 5,000 Polish people living in Ireland. About 300 of these are long term residents'*. At that point there were 273,000 Celtic Tiger immigrants living in Ireland, many of whom were Polish. The article was entitled *'Invasion of the job snatchers? Not likely'*. He quoted Izabela Grabowska of the Polish Embassy offering the opinion that *'we can expect maybe a few more thousand people but not hundreds of thousands'*. Ms Grabowska was only wide of the mark by a multiple of ten or twenty. A large proportion of the 66,000 (official arrivals) that came here in the year following the accession of the new member states (1 May 2004) were Poles and that was just the start. By the end of 2005, Polish nationals held 64,600 (CSO) of the 165,000 PPS numbers issued to migrants from the ten new accession states. In the same article Oliver Donohue of the ICTU and an unnamed European Commission official assured us that *'there won't be a serious influx of people'*. Perhaps this was a genuinely held belief, but if it was, it was seriously in error.

In another report referred to in an article entitled 'EU enlargement fears are unfounded, survey finds' in the *Irish Independent* 27th February 2004[(7)], a Dr Krieger is reported as saying the overall number of inward migrants is *'much less than predicted by some politicians'*. This was more wishful thinking or another prediction seriously wide of the mark.

The British Government of Tony Blair, prior to the granting of unfettered access in 2004, had received a report commissioned by the Home Office, referred to in an article in the *Irish Independent* in May 2004[8], that predicted, what proved to be, an utterly ridiculous annual influx of between 5,000 and 13,000 migrants a year from Eastern Europe into Britain, which ended up being more than ten times that number.

The overall effect of the media narrative on this fundamentally important issue, in both Ireland and Britain, was to play down the potential scale of the influx that was about to occur and to reassure the public that everything was under control. How anyone could seriously believe that migration to Western Europe would not be attractive to many in the accession states, is nothing short of ridiculous. This was naivety in the extreme or else a clumsy attempt to manipulate the public in the same vein as the 'Weapons of Mass Destruction', the infamous justification for British involvement in the war in Iraq. As with the 'Weapons of Mass Destruction' business, the consequences of granting 'unfettered access' were even more far-reaching for Britain. The mass migration episode that followed (after 1st May 2004), fuelled the general unease about migration policy and was a major component in the British decision to exit the EU.

Meanwhile, in Ireland, having committed to unfettered access two years previously and already having broken through the mass migration barrier, to the acclaim of a cheerleading media, government and business sector, there was no going back. The public were led to believe that what was happening was all good. The media narrative was almost all positive, with little mention of possible downsides to the far-reaching social and economic consequences of what we were letting ourselves in for.

When the barrier came down the flood into Ireland became a tsunami. Average income in Western Europe in 2004 was up to six times that of the accession states (European Advisory Group report 2004[9]), so the attraction was immense. Social welfare rates here were the equivalent of, or better than a good salary in Eastern

Europe. A good level of services like education and healthcare were virtually free and high housing costs could be mitigated by state assistance. For anyone with the inclination to move, Ireland was a better option than most. And so it proved, as borne out by the numbers arriving.

Meanwhile the Irish trade union movement was asleep at the wheel, tucked up between business and government in the social partnership bandwagon. At the time (2004), a report by the European Advisory Group (referred to earlier), said that enlargement would lead 'to greater unemployment across the Union'[9]. The report said that *greater wage flexibility would be essential'*, coded language for lower wages. It also noted that several studies would lead to a conclusion that *'enlargement will lead to migration of labour which will lead to downward pressures and possible unemployment'* in the original fifteen EU member countries. These conclusions should all have been red flashing lights for the trade union movement but were they ever even considered? Only Ireland, the UK and Sweden exposed themselves to this risk, the others refused access for up to seven years, having taken the Advisory Group's warning on board.

The conclusions of this report were hardly surprising. Anyone with a scrap of common sense could see that if you allow access to fifteen rich countries to workers from ten poor countries with 80 million inhabitants, a substantial flow will occur. That same European Advisory Group report quoted studies that forecast *'migration from the accession countries will run at between 1.2 and 5 per cent of their populations'*, which is between 1 and 4 million people. This is a lot of people, especially when it is divided between Ireland the UK and Sweden. It should have given the Irish trade union movement pause for thought, if they had their wits about them.

Ethics take a Back Seat

Hubris and folly were much in fashion in Ireland prior to the accession of the Eastern European states in 2004. When caution and prudence prevailed elsewhere, we jumped in with both feet. Working from the premise articulated in the media (*Irish Independent* 24th January 2006)[(10)] *that 'Ireland's population alone no longer has the capacity to sustain the economic boom'*, we allowed unfettered access to our labour market. The government, business and the trade unions never questioned, the worth, the desirability or the sustainability of the 'boom', to the Irish people as a whole. With eyes firmly fastened on their own interests, they went for the money.

The important ethical question that should have arisen at this point, for the EU, the Irish government and the trade union movement was, in a situation in an economy where there is virtually full employment, why encourage further activity, when there are ten other countries in the same group which are underdeveloped and poor? Ethics of course are all very well when wheeled in to support 'progressive' liberal objectives, but when they begin to interfere with money making activities and profits, it's time to call a halt.

Poland was by far the largest of the accession states, with a population of 38.6 million, nearly the same size as the other nine combined. In 2004 it had an unemployment rate of 19.1 per cent. Our government was anxious to solve a perceived labour shortage problem in the economy and was also anxious to facilitate the EU Commission, in its 'free movement of labour' agenda. These circumstances combined to convince the government that it was a good idea to grant access to people from the ten new member states.

For business this was a major stroke of good fortune. Access to an enormous pool of well educated, hard-working cheap labour was achieved with the minimum of red tape. It also introduced stiff competition to a tightening labour market.

In contrast, the situation for the trade union movement, their members and their families and workers in general, this move was almost entirely negative. Under the shadow of competition in the labour market, modest wage increases were agreed at social partnership level, even though the booming economic conditions would have warranted much higher levels of wages in a normal market. The economic cake was growing but labour's slice was shrinking in relative terms. Workers needed bigger incomes to keep pace with rising living costs, housing prices went through the roof and services deteriorated.

Apart from the effect on the existing workforce, the 170,000 unemployed would struggle to find work in a more competitive environment. They were soon joined on the dole queue by immigrants who failed to find work, all at the expense of the Irish taxpayer. This was a monumental blunder by the trade union movement that stopped the economic advancement of working people in its tracks and has led to a situation where living standards for most ordinary people are virtually static for the last decade.

4

The Irish Klondike

The 1980's were a period of stagnation and economic decline in Ireland. The very high levels of emigration that had plagued the country since the beginning of the twentieth century and indeed since the Famine of 1845, made an unwelcome return. The state registered the first fall in population since the 1950's in the 1991 census, following a prolonged recession.

But that was all about to change. The beginning of the nineties saw a glimmer of light that, by the end of the decade had turned into a raging inferno. Charlie Haughey's prediction of 'unprecedented prosperity' became a fact – at least for some. The rocket fuel of cheap money and cheap labour combined and spawned the Celtic Tiger.

A key element in the transformation of the Irish economy was company taxation policy. Low company tax was Ireland's contribution to the neoconservative revolution pioneered by Thatcher and Regan, that swept the world in the eighties. By adopting a 12.5 per cent corporation profits tax and a generous array of tax write-offs and loopholes, Ireland managed to suck up an enormous amount of the foreign direct investment that was looking for a secure and profitable home. Ireland led the way in a race to the bottom, unhindered by leftist or liberal scruples with regard to company taxation. And while we still lead the way in that department, it is a challenge that has been taken up by many others in recent times, to the great delight and satisfaction of the rich everywhere. The corporation tax rate has become an article of faith of Irish economic policy, a founding principle of the liberal consensus era, which we are prepared to defend with every fibre of our being, according to our former Taoiseach Enda Kenny! Despite shifting the taxpaying burden even more firmly onto working people, it has general acceptance right across the political spectrum, even to the far reaches of the left.

Wooed by the low corporation tax rate, an English-speaking workforce, access to the huge European market and the pro-business ethos here, many of the biggest multinational companies in the world, in the pharmaceutical, technology and healthcare areas set up operations here. While the EU looked on askance and talked of level playing fields, we cut the ground from under the competition in the tax stakes. The then Tánaiste, Mary Harney, speaking on 4th April 2004[(1)], was quoted in the media (*Irish Independent*) as saying, the Irish economy was built on the back of low tax rates and there was *'no question of throwing in the towel'*. This was in response to a comment by Paul McGowan (a senior tax partner with KPMG), to the effect that maybe the rate should be raised to 15 per cent, to placate the EU. He said he realised this could *'sound like national treason'*, and to the business elite, the Industrial Development Authority (IDA) and the government it did, so it was duly ignored. **(See Appendix 4)**

The booming multinational sector became the backbone of the economy with a large core of fairly well paid jobs and twice as many spin-off jobs. The 1980s cull of the old native industries was soon replaced by more vibrant, modernised and flexible enterprises and a host of small businesses. The revamped tourist industry, powered by competitive (cheap) migrant labour took off. A big motorway building programme was undertaken around the same time and infrastructure spending expanded, much of it coming from EU structural funds. The moribund construction sector came back to life and cheap credit turbocharged demand for housing. This was the Celtic Tiger economy. Phenomenal economic growth rates averaging 9.75 per cent were achieved during the late 1990s. An economic backwater on the edge of Western Europe was transformed into an Irish Klondike.

The Promised Land

Before long, the story got out that the streets of Ireland were paved with gold. But just as in Percy French's famous song *'The Mountains of Mourne'*, it wasn't quite true. Recruitment agencies – another great success story of the period – soon had a steady stream of clients making their way to the emerald isle from Eastern Europe and Asia. When they arrived in the period before EU enlargement, their new employers not only took delivery of their services but also of their work permits. This situation was referred to in a letter I received from Jack O'Connor on the 15th March 2004 where he said *'We (SIPTU) are also strenuous in our exposure of both Government and employers in operating a system of work permits which facilitates exploitation of immigrant workers by tying them to a particular employer and, because of a lack of freedom to move to a better job, keeping such workers trapped in low pay'*. This bound the migrant, hand and foot, to their new employer. The unfortunate migrant was thus tethered to a particular employer, who could then exert undue influence to a greater or lesser extent over their work, life and circumstances. To say that their position was akin to slavery would not have been an exaggeration in some cases. The situation for non-EU workers – requiring a work permit – appears to be little better today, if the deliberations of the Dail Joint Committee on Business Enterprise and Innovation are to be believed. In its Observations and Recommendations, dated 27th November 2018, it says *'the issue of work permits being tied to an employer can be particularly problematic for lower skilled, lower paid jobs'.*

No wonder some employers were so enthusiastic about migrant labour. The room for exploitation was endless and doubtless some took full advantage. Complaints were few, with the threat of revoking the work permit always in the background. Despite these drawbacks there was no shortage of takers. By the time EU enlargement took place in 2004 more than 273,000 had arrived.

To try to get some perspective on the scale of migration to Ireland over the last twenty-five years, it may be useful to make the comparison with the German migrant episode of late 2015. For the purposes of this book and as a convenient yardstick, I have adopted a definition of mass migration as 'a situation where the annual influx is greater than 1 per cent of the population of the country', which is what happened in Germany in 2015. The Biblical exodus from Turkey to the Promised Land of Europe in that year is now generally agreed to have been an episode of mass migration. The event is often referred to as *'the migrant crisis'.* These are terms that have never been used to describe what happened in Ireland, although the numbers, per capita, are much greater. This fundamental failure of perspective, whether deliberate or unintentional, has helped to produce the myopia that allows the elephant in the room that is mass migration to remain undetected, unnamed and ignored.

Germany has a population of 82.7 million people (2013 Sunday Times atlas), seventeen times the size of Ireland's population (4.9million) today. Back in 1996, at the beginning of the immigration influx, the population of Ireland was 1.3 million less at 3.626 million (CSO). That year more than 400 non-nationals a week came to live and work here, a total of 21,500 (CSO) or the equivalent of 0.6 per cent of the population at that time. The German pro-rata equivalent at the time would have been 500,000 people or more than half of the 2015 migrant crisis figure. While the Germans would rightly have viewed this substantial influx with concern, we in Ireland, back in 1996, were barely aware of it. The Irish media had either failed utterly to appreciate the significance of these numbers or were perhaps sold on the benefits of the societal transformation agenda, that was regarded as progressive. Either way, they failed to keep the Irish public informed of a fundamental change that was afoot, with profound implications for this country and its people.

The numbers arriving in Ireland continued at a similar level until the end of 1999. Many Irish nationals who had emigrated in the 1980's also returned during this period. The next year, 2000, there was a substantial increase in non-national immigration to 27,700 or more than 500 a week. At that stage (2000), according to *the UN International Migration Report 2017* there were 351,000 migrants (officially) resident in Ireland or 9% of the population, one third of whom (116,000) had arrived in the previous five years.

Despite the dot com bubble crash, the nine eleven terrorist attack in New York and a slowdown in the Irish economy, from 9.75 per cent growth to 5 per cent, the rate of migration into the country increased by another 20 per cent in 2001 to 32,800. It climbed again by more than 22 per cent in 2002 to 39,900 or to more than 1 per cent of the population of the state, breaching the mass migration threshold, a point at which, at the very least, alarm bells should have started ringing. At this juncture in 2015 the Germans were so alarmed at the Syrian influx, that they considered closing their borders, in contravention of the Schengen agreement. Instead of registering, at the very least, some concern at this situation, the Irish media narrative on the subject was how wonderful all this diversity was and how it was enhancing our lives.

The rate remained at around 42,000 a year for the next two years − an alarming 1 per cent plus of the population − until EU enlargement took place on 1st May 2004. This rapid demographic transformation, with its many profound, often negative implications, as it turned out later, was never critically analysed or examined in the media. We were sleepwalking into unknown territory and no-one was going to sound the alarm −because they hadn't noticed or because it might sound like racism. The anxiety about contravening politically correct boundaries had taken hold to such an extent − apparent in the David Begg letter quoted on page 41,42 − that the word 'migration' was now off limits.

The Flood Gates Opened

When unfettered access to the Irish and British labour markets finally became a reality for the ten new member states in Eastern Europe, the flood gates opened. Work permits were no longer required by citizens of these countries, wage rates were considerably higher than at home and jobs were plentiful. The migrant arrival numbers increased by 25,000 to 66,000 that year (May 2004-2005) or to 1.7 per cent of the Irish population, with 52,300 coming mainly from the accession states. That was a rate of 1,300(non-national) arrivals a week, for the entire year! The German pro-rata equivalent would have been 1.4 million people or nearly one and a half times the 2015 migrant crisis figure.

The failure of the media to appreciate what was happening or a reluctance to disturb the liberal consensus narrative, is well illustrated by Paul Melia's article in the *Irish Independent* on 2nd May 2005 [2] when he wrote *'Just 75,000 people from the 10 new EU member states have come to Ireland since accession on May 1 last year'* (the CSO figure was 52,300 from the accession states and 66,000 in all). He continued *'fears of a flood had failed to materialise'*! In fact what had happened was that the equivalent of almost one and a half times the numbers of migrants that had swarmed into Germany in 2015 had just arrived in Ireland. Of course he was not alone in his interpretation of the facts. Perhaps it is our generous nature that clouds our perception of scale, but most of our commentators, politicians and trade unionists seem to be particularly challenged in this regard. The flood had indeed arrived. What had failed was their ability to comprehend the difference between a high tide and a tsunami. Just how many migrants would the Irish media consider a flood? When this happened in Germany, ten years later, it shook the EU to its foundations. We know that the Germans, whether they supported the Merkel invitation or not, regarded this event as an episode of mass migration, a migrant crisis. We know that it has inflicted enormous damage on the EU and its structures, particularly Schengen. We know that it has seriously undermined trust in the European political system, the media and in democracy itself. It may yet prove to be the turning point at which the public lost confidence in the EU and its objectives.

That failure of the media in Ireland, which is undoubtedly what it was, to first of all comprehend what was happening, let alone analyse and forensically examine this major social and economic event, which would have disastrous consequences further down the track, is deeply troubling. It was a serious warning, if indeed one was needed, that ideology and partiality were beginning to infect and corrupt the truth. The political correctness malaise of the progressive liberal establishment had taken hold and was rewriting the news.

The next three years, with the barriers removed, saw huge numbers of non-nationals arriving, as was only to be expected in those circumstances. In 2006, the official figure for non-national migrants coming here to live and work was 88,900. That same year 20,000 returned home, so that the net figure was 68,200 (CSO). Instead of the deep concern that was appropriate, the situation was greeted with euphoria in the media. Headlines like 'Through the Roof' in the *Irish Independent* on 23 March 2006[3] greeted news of the waxing property bubble and the mass migration phenomenon that was supporting it. To those in a position to profit, it was indeed a great boon, a welcome addition to the customer base and a source of cheap labour.

All records for migration were broken in 2007. A total of 151,000 people arrived or 3,000 a week, 120,400 of whom were non-Irish. Around 33,000 returned giving a net extra 87,000 new non-national arrivals in the state (a full 2% of the Irish population) or the German equivalent of 1.65 million people. At this rate of change the native Irish would be in a minority within a generation or two and the longed for societal transformation that many 'progressives' yearned for would be achieved.

In 2008, the year of the crash, our popularity with the migrant remained undimmed. That year 89,700 non-nationals arrived and 35,900 departed, leaving a healthy 53,800 net gain of surplus labour, for the fast shrinking Irish economy. During all this time, apart from a few voices in the wilderness, no one challenged the conventional wisdom, the apparently universal consensus on the merits of overwhelming our society and economy with a flood of outsiders. Nobody dared to even suggest that there might be a downside to the hyper-expansion that might lead to collapse, despite the evidence of a thousand bubbles. The penny never dropped, as to the scale of this demographic transformation in the Irish media, or if it did, they were not going to trouble the Irish public by mentioning it.

So ended a seven year run of mass migration that changed the face of Ireland utterly. For seven years, from 2002 to 2008 inclusive, inward migration exceeded one per cent of the population every year and in at least two of those years by almost two per cent a year. No other country with any regard for the welfare of its citizens would tolerate such a situation for such a long period. A price would soon have to be paid. From a position where the country had fewer migrants than most European countries, we had charged up the migrant league table to the front. Yeats's prediction that 'a terrible beauty is born' was about to make a second coming, in a different guise.

The Triumph of Optimism

In just four years between 2005 and 2008 we had absorbed the German equivalent almost 5 million people as we teetered on the edge of an economic precipice. No wonder we had a hard landing. Even when the inevitable happened and we went over the edge, they still kept coming. An article in the *Sunday Independent* on 8th February 2009[4] explained why. It said that *'in the case of non-Irish nationals from Eastern Europe, being unemployed in Ireland could still present a more attractive option than a return to one's home country'*. This was because, it continued, *'jobseeker's benefit stands at over €200 per week here and matches – and in some cases outstrips – professional salaries'* at home. And so it proved.

In the first full year of the collapse, 2009, 50,600 non-nationals came here looking for work – or perhaps welfare – in a country of rocketing unemployment. Luckily, a slightly larger number – 52,800 departed – leaving our dreadful unemployment situation much the same. They continued to come, because we had missed the deadline in April 2006 for shutting the unfettered access door and, at that stage, the party was still in full swing and optimism and euphoria were overflowing. Worse still, the people we pay to inform and interpret the signs and call us to order when things get out of hand, were themselves intoxicated by the heady brew. Enthralled by notions of the rainbow nation, endless diversity and the cultural enhancement that it promised – to what once was a staid and colourless existence in a boring backwater – like the lotus eaters, the commentators and the pundits forgot all about the job in hand.

There were 441,689 people out of work in Ireland on average in 2010. That year, the worst of the recession, despite the financial meltdown, the continuing economic crisis and rising unemployment – 24,000 non-Irish arrived here on a totally incredible quest for work – or having been offered work! Just over 40,000 left the country that year, the only time in the last twenty three years that there was a substantial negative difference between non-national arrivals and those leaving. A not to be repeated, net 16,300 non-nationals left Ireland in 2010, a modest number compared to the host of arrivals in the previous few years.

As the crisis continued in 2011, compounded by the austerity programme agreed with the Troika and with unemployment at record levels of 444,906 people out of work and another 70,000 or so on training schemes, they continued to come. The inward migration of non-Irish was 33,700 during the year, almost enough to compensate for the outward bound figure of 38,600, leaving a small negative migration of 4,900.

The recession and austerity continued in 2012 and so did the continuous stream of immigrants. That year their unfailing optimism brought 32,200 non-nationals to our shores despite the 400,000 unemployed that were here already. Fortunately, 40,600 left, giving a small negative figure of 8,400. This was to be the last of four years where the numbers of non-nationals coming here were less than the leavers, in the twenty-three year period from 1996 to 2019.

The three-year Troika austerity programme was scheduled to end in December 2013 and there was the hope that a chink of light might appear at the end of the tunnel. One group who had never lost hope in the better life Ireland could provide were the migrants. Despite the continuing slack in the labour market at 419,000 unemployed, they continued to arrive in numbers that were beginning to grow again. In 2013 another 40,300 non-nationals came. There were 38,100 leavers in 2013, so there was a small positive figure.

By 2014 inward migration was growing strongly again with 9,000 more people arriving than in the previous year, bringing the total to almost 49,100. There were 41,200 leavers that year, giving a net figure of almost 8,000 extra non-nationals living and working here.

There was strong growth in the arrival numbers again in 2015, with a total of 57,100 arriving that year. This was 8,000 more than the previous year and established a strong and consistent growth trend in inward migration. For three years running now the number of non-nationals arriving here had increased by 8,000. The migrant arrival figure for 2015 was nearly twice the figure for 2012. Leavers amounted to 45,600 giving a net figure of 11,500 new permanent non-national residents in the state.

The number of non-Irish migrants arriving in 2016 was up slightly at 58,300 but the number of leavers was down very significantly at 34,400. This saw the net figure of new migrants remaining in the country more than double to 23,900 from the 11,500 net for the previous year. We were back to the inward migration levels of the late 1990s in the early Celtic Tiger period.

In 2017 this strong trend was maintained according to the CSO estimates. It believes that 57,200 non-Irish migrants arrived and 34,000 left, giving a net 23,200 additional non-national residents. More than half of those 57,200 new arrivals (29,400) were from outside the EU.

In 2018 the non-national migrant arrival figure was again up by almost 5,000 to 61,900 and departures were down by 6,000 to 28,000. The net non-national migration total rose to 33,900 or an astonishing 50% more than the previous year, maintaining the strong upward trend.

The most recent figures from the CSO [5] to April 2019 put non-national arrivals at 61,700 and departures at 25,900 to give a net figure of 35,800 new non-national residents in the state, up almost 2,000 on the previous year.

These are the official figures for the Irish inward migration phenomenon of the last twenty three years that has transformed the country. They are widely believed to be an underestimate. Back in 2007, in an article in the *Sunday Times* on 2nd September[6] the ICTU called for *'detailed research to establish the true number of overseas workers in Ireland'*. It said *'the census count of 11,000 Chinese immigrants in Ireland was far short of the 100,000 some observers have estimated are actually here'*. The same article states that *'the census recorded 63,000 Polish citizens in Ireland in April 2006, the Polish embassy has estimated that the real number could be as high as 200,000'*. An article in the *Irish Independent* on 1st November 2007[7] quoted Chambers Ireland and the Equality Authority as claiming that 17 per cent of the workforce was foreign when the CSO figure was 10 per cent. Another article in *The Sunday Times* on 7th April 2013[8] commenting on the accuracy of British migration figures from 2000 to that time (2013), claimed that the 3 million in the official figures had been joined by another million illegal immigrants over the period. It could well be the case in Ireland too, that a large number of immigrants just do not appear in official figures.

The truth is, we haven't a clue who is here because we do not require immigrants to register their addresses or carry identity papers as most other countries do. When Michael McDowell introduced 'The Immigration, Residence and Protection Bill 2007 to combat marriages of convenience and a requirement by non-EU citizens to carry identity papers, he was met by a storm of criticism from the Irish Council for Civil Liberties, the Irish Refugee Council, the Jesuit Centre for Faith and Justice and the Immigrant Council of Ireland, according to an article in the Irish Independent on 28th April 2007 by Dearbhail McDonald[9]. The Bill never became law, the farce continued and the Irish taxpayer paid up.

Sham marriages continue to be a problem, with the Gardai running 'Operation Vantage in 2016, identifying hundreds of such marriages in a short period, according to an article in the Sunday Times 30th October 2016[10]. Were the participants deported – highly unlikely.

A further indication of underestimated migration figures is the enormous number of PPS numbers issued to migrants. Foreign nationals made 920,000 applications for PPS numbers between 2002 and 2007[11], while the official arrivals figure was around 400,000. Some of this is accounted for by short-term stayers but did half a million return? This stretches the bounds of credibility.

Whether we believe the official figures or take the view that they are seriously underestimated, as many believe they are, the fact remains that even the official figures are staggering. This is indeed a remarkable story, in numbers, of how we came from being a country with relatively low numbers of migrants, to having one of the highest migrant densities in Europe.

It is also the story of how a modest recovery, after a painful recession in the 1980s, was hijacked by unbridled greed, that turned sustainable progress into a bloated economic disaster waiting to happen, which in time, it duly did. It is the story of how cheap labour, in large quantities, was harnessed to generate great wealth for a business elite, who soon lost the run of themselves. It is the story of how the media acted as cheerleader-in-chief for this folly, in the name of 'progressive life enhancing' diversity, when they should have been pointing out the pitfalls and calling out the madness. It is the story of how, when the gold rush was over, the cheap labour tap couldn't be turned off and almost submerged the economy, leaving a lot of fiscal and economic damage and social and cultural disruption.

Official Migrant Arrivals and Departures (CSO)

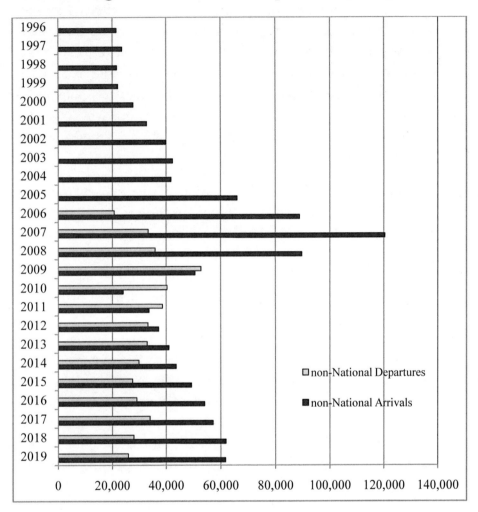

Fig. 4-1 Shows the growing number of arrivals in the Celtic Tiger period (1996 to 2008), the three-year period after the crash when arrivals almost matched departures and the resumption of strong growth in net arrival numbers since 2012 (Figures gleaned from CSO releases).

The migration tap is still running and the pressure is beginning to build up again. If the trend of the last seven years continues and there is every indication that it will, Ireland will soon see a return to the mass inward migration of the Celtic Tiger period, where net migrant numbers exceed one per cent of the population each year. We are already three quarters of the way there and with business organisations calling for increased 'flexibility' with regard to work-permit issue and increased inward migration, mass migration will be back sooner rather than later. Hot on its heels will come the associated problems of ever-tightening housing shortages and deteriorating public services.

While the prohibition on discussion of the subject remains steadfastly in place here, the migration question is the subject of a great debate both in Europe and America. It is dominating public discourse and effecting fundamental political change in many European countries and is likely to continue to do so, in the near future. It needs to be vigorously and honestly debated in Ireland too and not just within the confines of political correctness. For this to happen, the stranglehold of the 'progressive' elite on public discourse must be broken. This will not happen easily, as can be seen in the furious reaction of the equivalent 'progressive' elements to the Trump presidency in the US and Brexit in Britain and in the West generally. Not satisfied with censoring discussion of immigration on the main stream media, 'progressive' liberalism appears to be setting its sights on shutting down opposing views on social media and the internet.

Holding the line on Free Movement

The Irish Government, if it were not in thrall to political correctness, should have made some attempt to prevent, or at least discourage the large numbers of migrants who continued to arrive on our shores, after the crash. We should, at the very least, have attempted to prohibit or restrict the payment of social welfare to claimants among the more than 180,000 migrants that arrived in Ireland in the five-year period after the crash. While our rich neighbours on the continent were sheltering behind the restricted access to their labour market, that they had the good sense to avail of in 2004, we were being hung out to dry. Not only did we have to allow access to large numbers of immigrants from the accession states, through our own foolishness, but we had to pay them as well, under an EU non-discrimination rule.

While the free movement of people was sacrosanct to the EU, an article in *The Irish Times* on 12 August 2011[12] reported that the European Union executive had agreed to allow Spain to restrict Romanians from seeking employment on its territory, citing the need to protect its labour market. Employment commissioner Laszlo Andor said *'This decision has been taken because of the very specific employment situation in Spain'*, in a statement. If the Spaniards succeeded in protecting their labour market why did Ireland not do the same? After all we had more than 400,000 on the dole at the time. But, perhaps being good Europeans was more important to our government than looking after the people's interests, so we did nothing. Meanwhile thousands of non-nationals from inside and outside the EU were allowed to swarm onto our dole queues.

The Irish political establishment which continued to run the country after the crash – the name plate changed from Fianna Fail to Fine Gael in 2011 but the policies remained essentially the same – were not just interested in being good Europeans but were also anxious to be seen as open-minded with regard to others as well. As proof positive of this, they were prepared to allow large numbers of migrants from outside the EU to enter and take up residence in the country at the height of our economic debacle. In the period 2009 to 2013 when Ireland was on its knees economically, 62,000 non-Irish non-EU migrants took up residence in the state, people to whom we had no obligation, good, bad or indifferent. Some of these people may have emigrated subsequently but many of them undoubtedly became a burden on the taxpayer, or if they had jobs to go to, why were some of the 400,000 people on the dole not given those jobs, or trained to do them?

Much of the cost of financing the social welfare bill for the huge numbers on the dole had to be borrowed and now forms part of the astronomical national debt that we have to live with for the foreseeable future and will burden generations to come. That bill and the substantial interest due on it, of €6 to 7 billion a year, at the current historically low interest rates, which amounts to €3,000 per year per employee, will be paid for by Irish workers and their families in higher taxes and poorer services. The progressive elite who set the political, social and economic agenda that led to the debacle, guided by the tenets of political correctness, continue to call the shots.

The principal beneficiaries of large-scale migration, apart from the migrants themselves, are the business elite. Importing a pliant, flexible and cheap workforce, whose skills match exactly their requirements, and dispensing with the tiresome and expensive task of training and educating the natives, makes a lot of sense to employers. The government no longer seems to regard its primary task as being the servant of all the citizens of the nation, but instead, as a facilitator of the global free market. As such, it cannot countenance or condone any hindrance to the free flow of capital, goods, services or indeed people in the service of the market. The migrant rush from Eastern to Western Europe that almost capsized our economy is of no concern to the market. Our government, in its thrall, dare not raise any objection to its activities, on pain of exclusion. How many times have we heard the mantra 'we are a small open economy' with the implicit threat that we had better behave ourselves, conform to the market's requirements, or else.

The fear, in government and state agencies, of upsetting big business and the multi-national corporations, by tightening work permit issue and skilled worker migration into Ireland is allowing big business and the multi-nationals to set the rules of migration policy. The former state training agency FAS was spending €1 billion of taxpayers money annually, much of it wasted, for very little return in terms of providing skilled workers for the needs of the Irish economy. The third level institutions seem also to have missed the mark in their efforts to match graduate output to the requirements of the economy. The end result appears to be that employers have to import skilled workers and specialists from outside the country, with the advantage of few training costs or effort for themselves, while the drawbacks, are shared out among the indigenous community. The reasonable expectation, that Irish people on the dole should be trained-up and reskilled wherever possible is thus dispensed with. There is no point in establishing industries or activities here if the workforce has to be imported. It only adds to pressure on infrastructure, housing and services and lowers the quality of life for everyone, particularly the less well off.

Like the original Klondike of 1897 and its swarm of prospectors, Ireland proved very attractive to a huge contingent of workers from Eastern Europe and elsewhere in the Celtic Tiger period. As in the Klondike, huge fortunes were made and lost by a small privileged minority on the back of this prolonged mass migration episode. The people who fared worst in the Klondike, were the original inhabitants of the area, the Han people, who were unceremoniously removed to a reservation where many died of diseases brought in by the new-comers. They were left with the wreckage, when the event was over, as were the Irish people in the aftermath of crash in 2008. At least in the Klondike when the gold rush was over many of the prospectors left the area. This will not be the case in Ireland. A housing crisis that will continue to grow with the continuing influx, poorer health and education services, the welfare system under pressure, static living standards for many and an enormous national debt are but part of the legacy of the Irish Klondike. The negative consequences of this episode for the less well-off will persist for many years.

5

Implosion

The epic tale of the Great Influx into Ireland that continues to this day and indeed, appears to be gaining momentum once again, is almost matched by the spectacular story of the fall of the Celtic Tiger. Having undermined the financial stability of our economy by reckless, risky and grossly excessive borrowing and lending, our financial institutions teetered on the brink of bankruptcy in the Autumn of 2008. When the sub-prime mortgage tsunami crossed the Atlantic and came crashing over their heads, they were left gasping and clutching at straws. Luckily for them, the Irish taxpayer was close at hand and at much cost to him and herself, managed to haul them ashore. The economy was badly damaged but the hero of the hour, the taxpayer, fared even worse. He and she suffered life altering injuries.

By 2007 the Celtic Tiger had run out of steam. After eleven years of phenomenal growth, which inevitably proved to be unsustainable, it had reached the top of the mountain and there was nowhere to go but down. Apart from the demographic transformation, the most remarkable aspect of the Celtic Tiger period was the growth in property sector output and prices. The property market bubble had grown to enormous proportions just before the crash and lay stranded, like a beached whale, helplessly awaiting its fate. When the US banking crisis rock punctured the global financial system, the Irish property bubble imploded. The number of house completions halved from 2006 to 2008 and halved again the following year. The 275,000 workers in the construction industry went on lean times or on the dole and a vital pillar of the Celtic Tiger economy collapsed.

Wall Street hit the buffers in September 2008 with the Lehman Brothers collapse and the red lights went on in the financial system worldwide. Within two weeks the Irish banking sector was in crisis and the government and their top officials were seized with panic. Over that last weekend of September 2008 they were persuaded that the banks were in imminent danger of collapse. The solution they came up with, after a sleepless night of frantic deliberations, was that the Irish Government would guarantee the deposits in Irish banks. In other words, the taxpayer would shoulder the burden and the risk of financial Armageddon.

As the crisis developed it became clear that many of the biggest clients of the Irish banks were involved in the speculation that had created the property bubble and when it collapsed they were unable to service their gigantic loans. The banks were swamped with impaired loans, credit dried up and with it consumer demand. While the financial institutions teetered on the brink of bankruptcy, their ability to lend and the ocean of cheap money they had borrowed from Europe disappeared overnight. A second pillar of the Celtic Tiger economy had collapsed.

These two events were linked in a domino effect but the circumstances which gave rise to the property bubble and the financial recklessness which flourished in the Celtic Tiger period would never have occurred but for the advent of mass migration. The sudden expansion of the population created an unprecedented demand for accommodation. The market responded with the building boom, which was sustained and enhanced by the accession of the ten new members of the EU and the flood of inward migration which followed in 2004 and in the following years. When unfettered access was granted to our labour market and our social welfare system, the effect was like opening a valve on an 80 million storage tank of cheap labour. A huge amount of demand was created in the economy as the population rocketed during the 1996 to 2011 period, by a remarkable 27 per cent!

But the domino effect started by the property collapse was not finished yet. The steep fall in house completions had a devastating effect on the public finances. Value Added Tax (VAT) and Stamp duty on the phenomenal number of house completions between 2004 and 2008 (380,000 houses were built in the period), distorted exchequer receipts, giving a false sense of buoyancy. Government budgets may have been constructed on the basis that this would continue indefinitely, which, if it were the case was extremely foolish. Foolish or not, the general consensus among the leading banking and financial analysts, media commentators and a large part of the general public, was that the pace of house building would continue at these very high rates for another ten to fifteen years[1]. The unanimous verdict was that the army of migrants required to fuel the Celtic Tiger economy, would continue to arrive in their droves and would be housed by a buoyant property sector, delivering massive wealth to its owners in the form of profits on sales of houses, capital appreciation and rental income. This preposterous scenario could not just be put down to the wishful thinking of the property sector in Ireland and their financial backers. It presumably was shared by the European financiers who provided the €100 billion to the banks, which was used to partially finance the bubble.

The collapse in the building trade and the stamp duty take and a number of other negative factors holed the public finances below the waterline. In 2007 there was a small surplus of about half a billion but by 2008 the public finances had nose-dived to a €13 billion deficit. The following year 2009 the deficit doubled again to a frightening €22.8 billion, a cumulative €36 billion in just two years. The economy was in meltdown. This indicated that we were spending 40 per cent more than we were taking in – a recipe for financial and economic disaster. The EU financial stability guideline was that the spending deficit should not exceed 3 per cent of GDP. Irish public finances were in serious crisis and required immediate radical surgery.

In 2010 the public finances disaster went completely off the scale. Receipts were €55.4 billion and expenditure was €109.1 billion, leading to a massive €53.7 billion deficit (CSO statistical release 13th July 2016). That year we spent twice what we took in and we were in economic catastrophe territory. This was due to the general economic and financial collapse, falling income tax, VAT, stamp duty, excise and corporation tax receipts and increased expenditure, particularly on social welfare. The banking crisis costs and these deficits when added together and combined with hefty deficits in 2011, 2012, and 2013 built up to an enormous government debt of over €200 billion. It is now eleven years since the crash and the debt hasn't changed much but we are managing to pay the €6 to 7 billion annual interest bill on it. Luckily for us, we are in a historically low interest rate environment.

The implosion of the property bubble, the banking crisis and the collapse of the public finances created the perfect storm for the Irish economy and brought the Celtic Tiger period to an ignominious end. Now the price would have to be paid, not by those responsible for the debacle but by the ordinary taxpayers who gained nothing by the folly and reckless exuberance of the episode.

Irish Government Revenue and Expenditure in € billions

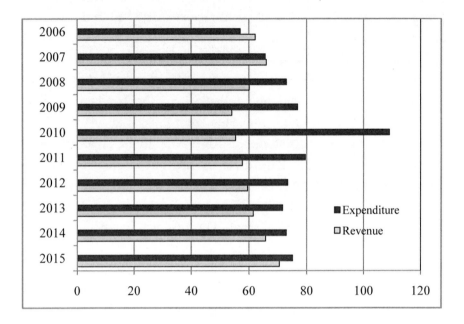

Fig. 5-1 Chart shows expenditure and revenue in € billions (source CSO statistical release 13 July 2016 Government income and Expenditure 2010-15 and the Department of Finance). A huge gap opened up between expenditure and revenue after 2007 amounting to €140 billion over the following eight years, which, when added to the pre-existing national debt stood at €198 billion in 2017.

The Banks

There was a widespread belief among house buyers in the 1980s and 90s that the Irish banks and building societies were operating a cosy cartel in their sector, to the detriment of their customers. It was assumed that the margin between the interest rates charged by the big international wholesale banks to the retail banks here and the rates they in turn charged to customers were excessive.

Competition was brought in to resolve the problem. Since the crash of 2008 that competition has almost disappeared again and margins have been allowed to increase again, to prop up the viability and reserves of the Irish financial institutions, to the cost of bank customers. So much, for competition and regulation. We now appear to be back to the situation that pertained in the 1980s.

Whatever can be said about banks and the conduct of their business, the bottom line is that they are not a social service. They exist to make a profit, first and last. It was up to the government to temper their commercial instincts by appropriate legislation and regulation and this it spectacularly failed to do. The atmosphere in the Celtic Tiger period became increasingly akin to the Wild West as far as banking was concerned. The law was held in contempt and the sheriff was asleep on the top deck of the Central Bank of Ireland. Recklessness, aggression and intense competition were the order of the day. The banks had been driving with the pedal to the floor, in a race with each other for market share. Their international bond borrowings had grown from €16 billion in 2003 to around €100 billion in 2007 and the money was being used to fund the increasingly precarious property bubble. When the bubble burst in 2008 many of the borrowers went bankrupt and were in no position to repay their loans.

Of all the examples of gross incompetence in the Celtic Tiger catalogue, and there are many, the prize for the most incompetent has to go to the Central Bank of Ireland. That institution, to the public at least, appeared to be packed with well-paid bureaucrats who beavered away at their desks doing God knows what for years, while the financial sector completely lost the run of themselves. No doubt, under instruction from the powers that be, perhaps in the Department of Finance, they implemented what came to be known as a regime of 'light regulation'. It was so light that it appears to have consisted of no more than a few meetings, where officials had the wool pulled over their eyes, perhaps a few lunches and a game or two of golf. Meanwhile the banks broke all the rules and engaged in reckless and risky behaviour.

When the inevitable happened and the whole thing came crashing down, civil service rules were applied and some of the individuals at the top were pensioned off, at considerable expense to the taxpayer. The catastrophic failure on behalf of the Central Bank of Ireland to police the financial institutions was a major factor in precipitating and deepening the Great Recession in Ireland.

The banking crisis rumbled on in 2009 with a partial recapitalisation, but it plumbed unprecedented depths in 2010. The nationalisation of Anglo Irish Bank and the recapitalisation of Allied Irish Bank (AIB) and a number of others cost the state €62.8 billion, almost a third of the National Debt. The expiry of the bank guarantee scheme in October 2010 precipitated a funding crisis which required massive borrowing on the bond markets. The rates at which the Irish Government could borrow – approaching junk bond rates of around 7 per cent – were unsustainable, so recourse had to be made to the European Central Bank (ECB). By the end of November the government was forced to accept a bailout of €85 billion by the ECB, the IMF and the European Commission, collectively known as the Troika.

At the beginning of 2009 three major elements of the recession were in place or emerging and at work undermining the Irish economy. The property bubble implosion after a period of stagnation in 2007-8 started the ball rolling. This helped to precipitate the banking crisis which followed hot on its heels. The public finances meltdown was an inevitable consequence of the first two hammer blows. The next disaster on the agenda was mass unemployment.

Mass Unemployment and Mass Migration

Throughout the late Celtic Tiger period the live register of unemployed remained around the 155,000 mark, which when training and back to work schemes are included brought the figure up to 210,000.The live register number for those out of work rose from 154,319 unemployed in 2007 to 195,598 in 2008, despite an increase of 11,000 in the number of people at work. This was a significant increase of 26 per cent (or 41,279) in the jobless numbers at a time when jobs were still being created in the economy. Part of the explanation for this, was that 1,000 to 2,000 migrants a week were arriving in Ireland at the time, many of whom were failing to find employment and signing on the dole.

Unemployment in the aftermath of the Crash

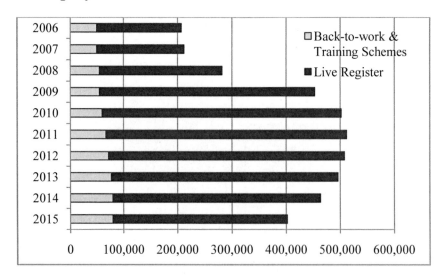

Fig. 5-2 The chart shows the unemployment (live register and back-to-work & training schemes) crisis after the crash (source CSO). Between 450,000 and more than half a million of our just over two million workforce were unemployed for six years after the crash.

By the time the leading edge of the Great Recession, in the form of the financial crisis had washed up on our shores in 2008, we had been joined by another enormous contingent of 89,700 immigrants. Many of these also joined the 195,598 already on the dole in the spring of 2008. When we went over the cliff in September 2008 the figure on the live register had reached 240,217. From that point onwards the numbers rocketed. The 800 people a week joining the dole queues in 2007-8 turned into more than 8,000 a week in early 2009. By the spring of 2009 there was a whopping total of 381,876 signing on. In addition to that figure there were another 55,000 on training and back to work schemes making the real figure closer to 440,000. This figure was twice the number for the year before and it was getting worse.

We found ourselves in the utterly farcical situation where huge job losses were being compounded by a biblical influx of migrants who had no prospect of finding employment here. No attempt was made by government to stem the influx − in fact quite the opposite. In January 2009, the worst month for job losses of the Great Recession when 35,000 jobs were lost, the Department of Enterprise, Trade and Employment issued 730 work permits, not to EU citizens but to people from outside the EU, to whom we had no obligation in terms of free movement. When decisive action was called for, the government seemed paralysed, unwilling or unable to act. Nor was any attempt made by the media to call attention to the catastrophic incompetence of the authorities in this regard. This was another indication of the extent to which the prohibition on any negative comment on migration had become embedded.

Between 2006 and 2011 the number of non-nationals at work increased by 23,700 (9.7%) according to a press release from the CSO [2]. However, the net number of new non-national arrivals (arrivals minus departures) over the same period was 190,500. This means that 88 per cent of the arrivals between 2006 and 2011 failed or did not attempt to find employment, which was hardly surprising in an economy in meltdown. That was, incredibly, seven out of every eight of those new arrivals or 167,000 people, who were dependant or unemployed.

This gives an indication of the extent of the probable social welfare tourism phenomenon in Ireland at the time. Presumably these individuals had come here on the off-chance of finding work, but whether they found work or not, they were better off in Ireland on social welfare than they were at home. While it may have been the logical course of action from their point of view, it was a terrible imposition on the Irish taxpayer and should not have been tolerated. It is a good illustration of why nations should have secure borders and the right to restrict entry. However, Irish Government and official incompetence had not changed since the fall of the Celtic Tiger, so nothing was done to put a stop to this blatant abuse.

The number of people on the live register in the spring of 2011 was 439,571. There were about 75,000 on training or work schemes – making a total of about 515,000 out of work and on social welfare. The vast majority of people who lost their jobs were private sector workers. This was a crushing weight on the economy, after three years of swingeing austerity.

The National Recovery Plan

Even before the collapse, the public finances had been struggling. The enormous job losses at the end of 2008 and early 2009 led to a steep fall in revenue from the income taxes of the one fifth of the workforce who were now unemployed and the VAT receipts from their reduced purchasing power. Expenditure on social welfare in the same period rose from €15.1 billion to €20.5 billion with 'Working Age Supports' almost doubling to €6.3 billion due to the steep rise in unemployment. The economic collapse was in full swing and the gap between income and expenditure was €23 billion. Something had to be done and quickly. The lead-in to the ECB bailout at the end of 2010 soon concentrated minds and provided the sombre climate required to swallow the harsh medicine that had to be taken. Hot on the heels of the bailout, the National Recovery Plan was published, prompted no doubt by the Troika, who were here to oversee our economic management in the crisis.

The National Recovery Plan outlined in detail how the economy was to be put back on its feet and where the €15 billion – in savings and tax hikes – required to bridge the gulf between income and expenditure would be found. The hatchets were sharpened and the cutting of current spending to the tune of €7 billion began, which included some staff numbers and pension adjustments in the public service and the health service. Capital spending was also cut. A further €7 billion would be collected in taxes, including income tax, property tax, carbon tax, VAT and an outrageous retrospective raid on private sector pension savings in the form of a levy. The measures would be introduced over the four-year duration of the plan and would operate for the foreseeable future. Irish workers and their families would shoulder the burden for the debacle, while corporation tax stayed at 12.5 per cent and the boom-time beneficiaries remained largely unscathed.

The financial crisis was a global event from which there was no escape. The particular set of circumstances that we found ourselves in, which were largely of our own making, made the crisis here a lot worse. A catalogue of bad decisions, gross incompetence and reckless actions brought us to the brink of destruction. Chief among these was the failure to control our borders and the decision to allow a huge influx of migrants into the country, which triggered a hyper-expansionary chain reaction in the economy. From that single circumstance sprang many of the ills that beset us, prior to and in the aftermath of the crash and are still with us today.

Diversity in Adversity

In 2002 when the Irish Government embarked on the reckless, uncharted course of unfettered access for the ten applicant countries from Eastern Europe, of course there were other elements to the decision apart from the economic ones. The loudest voices in Irish society, the first citizens of the progressive elite were convinced of the merits of more and deeper diversity. This was an opportunity to build on progress already made in freeing up our moribund mono-cultural backwater, and creating, in their view, a vibrant, open and diverse society. Multiculturalism was all the rage at the time and the progressive liberal element was keen to push for societal transformation, in the likeness and image of what they regarded as the most advanced societies of Britain and the United States.

The decision to allow unfettered access was taken mainly to facilitate the labour requirements of employers but it also indulged the fashionable multicultural aspirations of 'progressive' liberalism. While it successfully satisfied these two requirements, unfortunately in doing so, it set us irrevocably on the road to economic disaster and to possible social upheaval in the future.

The failure to question, probe and forensically interrogate the unfettered access issue was no surprise to any observer of the media and politics in Ireland. The 'group-think mentality' and its cuddly counterpart 'consensus', that dominated the media, had bought into the idea of the open door policy and were also in a position to silence dissent. They had already decided what was best for us and had spent the previous five years cheer-leading the country down the shining path to multiculturalism. By the mid noughties a well-established conditioning process was in place. Every television programme, news item and advertisement had a multicultural flavour. Dozens of happy clappy articles regularly appeared in print and broadcast outlets, extolling the virtues of 'diversity' and its enriching effect on culture, society and the economy. The political correctness credo had taken over. There was no need for debate – the decision had already been made.

By the time the Great Recession struck, after ten years of 'consensus' and conditioning, we had been convinced that there was no alternative to the open door policy, to the globalised labour market. It didn't seem to enter our heads that we should close the door, or at least try to. When unemployment rocketed, there was no clamour in the media or indeed elsewhere, to close the floodgates. The house was being swamped before our eyes by a tsunami of unemployment, compounded by large-scale immigration, yet our commentariat said nothing. It was plain to see that the extraordinary period of massive inward migration that had preceded the crash had unhinged the economy. Yet nothing was said about this major element in the debacle. The crucial connection between mass unemployment and mass immigration was never made. And that remains the case to this day.

Ireland of the Cead Mile Failte

The media reluctance to adequately analyse the circumstances, actions and policy failures that had deepened the economic crisis in Ireland and the crucial connection with inward migration was consistent with the ideology that now dominated public discourse. The Irish media were the standard-bearers for the agenda that was pursued in the Celtic Tiger period. They were a crucial part of the consensus that ruled the roost.

While comment and critical analysis of the underlying reasons were in short supply, there was plenty of reportage on the economic crisis itself, shedding some light on the lack of urgency with which it was managed. A report in the *Sunday Independent* on 8th February 2009[(3)], six months into the Great Recession, revealed that the number of people on the dole the previous month was 327,860. The number was expected to hit at least 400,000 by year end. It also informed us that 2,000 foreign nationals a week were coming to Ireland *'in search of jobs'*. The previous month the Department of Enterprise, Trade and Employment, ignoring those on the dole, issued 730 work permits to people from outside the EU (as mentioned previously) to whom we had no obligation. In the same article, a department spokesman, when asked if there were any plans to tighten up the rules for work permits – after all we were six months into the worst economic crisis since the Second World War – said that certain parts of the scheme were currently being examined. He added that there could be some changes to *'administrative arrangements'*, but that the review was at an early stage.

He did not say the department was going to stop the flood of immigrants or halt the issue of work permits. Presumably there were still jobs for non-EU nationals in the Irish economy. He did, however, go on to explain that the introduction of an English language competency – these were probably the *'administrative arrangements'* referred to earlier – as a criterion for getting an employment permit, could pose difficulties. This government department was obviously prepared to issue work permits to non-English speaking migrants from third countries, who would like to come here to work in the middle of an employment crisis. This was indeed generosity above and beyond the call of duty.

Surely this was a situation where investigative journalism could have had a field day, probing and investigating the circumstances surrounding the issue of work permits and why the huge cohort of unemployed were not retrained to fill any available vacancy. The continuing migrant influx in a catastrophic unemployment crisis, should have been the subject of continuous scrutiny in the media, until effective measures were taken to put a stop to it. None of this happened of course, because official incompetence was matched by media reticence in the matter of calling for a halt to a flood of inward migration that would end up on the dole queues. The media

group-think consensus on immigration control held firm, even
the height of the crisis. Government officials were probably awa
that had they attempted to halt the influx, an almighty hue and c
about discrimination would have arisen.

In any event nothing was done and the influx continued. The
Minister for Enterprise, Trade and Employment had other more
important concerns than the problems of the unemployed or the
burden on the tax-payer. The British had reportedly brought in a
raft of immigration restrictions, including a requirement to prove
that a suitable employee could not be found in the European
Economic Area (EEA) before a permit was granted but could an
Irish government afford to do that? Fear has always been the
driving force behind our thinking on immigration policy. The
business lobby and the multinationals wouldn't like it.

If it was the case in 2009 that suitably qualified people could
not be found, out of a half a million unemployed, then what were
the planners, FAS and the Minister for Education doing to rectify
the situation? Indeed, what have they done in the intervening
eleven years? The Irish taxpayer is due to spend €11.2 billion on
education this year (2020). Is it too much to ask that our third level
educational institutions should design the array of courses they
offer to meet the requirements of our economy? After all, this is
not an entertainment budget for our post-secondary young people
or some kind of right-of-passage to adulthood. Nor is it a financial
facility for indulging the whims of the academic community. Hard
pressed, hard-working people, most of whom have never stood
inside the gate of a third level institution, are paying a lot of
money for this. There should be no question of having to bring in
people from outside to fill vacancies, except in very exceptional
cases.

The average number of people on the Live Register in 2010 was
441,689 with more than 60,000 on back-to-work schemes, almost
two years after the crash. By 2011 it was 444,905 and it remained

around this figure for the next two years falling slowly thereafter. Undeterred by the deep unemployment crisis in the country, the immigrants continued to come. No matter what happened in the employment stakes for non-nationals, they were better off here than at home. Irish wage rates were far above rates available at home and more to the point social welfare rates here, plus extra assistance, were also a good deal better than paid employment in the ten accession states, where most of our migrants came from (see chart below). For people from most third countries the advantages of being here were far greater again.

The average (before tax) wage in Ireland in 2017 (Wikipedia 2017) was €3050 per month gross, while the average in Poland was €991/m, in Latvia it was €836/m, in Lithuania it was €793/m, in Estonia it was €1,119/m, in the Czech Republic it was €1,008/m, in Slovakia it was €901/m and in Hungary it was €992/m. Average wages in some African countries are less than €100/month. Unemployment benefit for an adult in Ireland is approximately €812/month and an array of other assistance is available through the social welfare system. Back in 2004 the differential was much greater, as was the incentive for citizens of the accession states to move to Ireland.

Average Income differential between Western & Eastern Europe

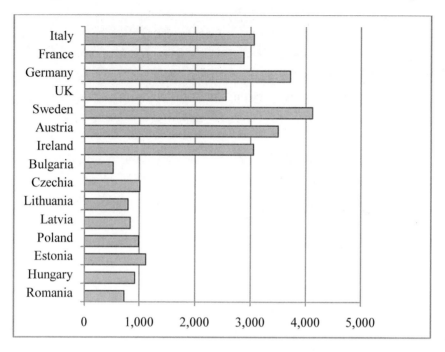

Fig. 5-3 The chart shows the monthly average gross wage in euro in 15 European countries in 2016 (source Wikipedia 2017). Wages in Eastern European countries are still only one third of Western European rates. When most Eastern European states joined the EU in 2004 the differential was much greater.

The Media issues a Fatwa

As the realisation dawned on the general public after 2004 that all the reassurances about low levels of immigration from government, business, the trade unions and the media were at best pure nonsense, people became anxious about the sheer volume of arrivals into the country. By the end of 2005 four out of five Irish people had real fears about the massive influx[4]. The evidence of mass migration was plain to be seen in every town and village in

Ireland. Between one and two thousand migrants a week were arriving from the time of the EU enlargement in May 2004 until after the crash in 2009. When the penny finally dropped with the politicians – who had ignored the public concern up to then – in January 2006, Pat Rabbitte and Ned O'Keeffe rather timidly mentioned that there was concern in the public mind about the levels of immigration. They were immediately rounded upon in the media.

Taking his cue from Joseph O'Malley in the Sunday Independent[5] two days previously, Sam Smyth in the *Irish Independent* on 24 January 2006, in an article entitled *'Fears over foreign workers coming here are misguided'*[6], lectured Pat Rabbitte and Ned O'Keeffe at length, for articulating the fears of an *'historically insecure workforce'*. The sub-heading of the article was *'Kindling the fears of an historically insecure workforce paid electoral dividends'*. Smyth accused *'those who should know better'*, presumably Rabbitte and O'Keefe, of feeding *'on the irrational fears'* of *'insecure workers'* and suggested that it *'is an extremely dangerous and irresponsible pitch'*, which Rabbitte and O'Keefe might have been prepared to exploit for electoral gain. Mr. Smyth was, and is, a leading member of the journalistic profession, whose views were fairly typical of those held by his peers and provides a good example of media thinking at the time. He presumably believed there was little merit in those fears and proceeded to rubbish them by allocating them the status of 'a fella told me in a pub' anecdote. **(For the full text of the article see Appendix 5)**

Mr. Smyth went on to draw a number of conclusions in regard to the concerns expressed by the two politicians. He appeared to believe that those concerns were *'the irrational fears of historically insecure workers'*. He also concluded that *'There is a readymade market of anti-immigrant xenophobes prepared to use the politicians' respectability as currency for their prejudice'*.

Putting two and two together, were irrationally insecure workers also anti-immigrant xenophobes? His contention that *'Any party, or politicians, who can harness the fear-of-foreigners vote can expect a corresponding electoral bonus'*, seems to indicate a belief on his part, that there was a large latent, anti-immigrant, xenophobic number of irrationally fearful voters around. If this was true, then it is rather surprising that it is not part of the policy platform of all the political parties in the state.

Unfortunately, the first impulse in Irish journalism, when the unalloyed merits of immigration are questioned, is to reach for the 'anti-immigrant xenophobia' brush, to tar the culprit with. Was voicing the concerns of the vast majority of Irish workers at the prospect of inviting 300,000 foreign workers into the country, pandering to their anti-immigrant xenophobic prejudices? Was this suggesting that anyone believing that large-scale inward migration was a serious concern – and that was four fifths of the Irish population, according to this article – was an irrational, prejudiced anti-immigrant xenophobe? Let's hope not.

Mr. Smyth agreed that politicians have *'an obligation to ventilate the genuinely held fears of their constituents'*, but not, it seemed, if it questioned the large scale immigration of 300,000 foreign workers. He qualified this obligation by saying *'there is an even greater responsibility to calm irrational views'*. And presumably this greater responsibility took precedence over the articulation of the genuinely held fears of the majority, because those fears were irrational. Having deemed those fears 'irrational', they could be conveniently dispensed with.

The concern about large-scale immigration – and at the time, at 1500 a week, it was large scale – soon proved to be all too rational. Unfortunately, within a very short space of time, these fears became the nightmarish reality of an imploding economy, mass unemployment and societal disruption.

This article could have been written by any number journalists in the mainstream media at the time. It's invitation to us, to accept *'the accumulated wisdom of the economists and others'* in relation to the management of the economy, was at odds with the fundamental principles of good journalism. The requirement to report the facts and inform the public, even if they don't fit in with your view of the world, is central to the role of journalism, in the first instance. Secondly, it must then question, analyse and interrogate in the pursuit of truth, not in support of some agenda, no matter how 'progressive'. On this important issue, Irish journalism has been failing in its duty to report, inform and analyse objectively for many years. The supporting role of journalism in the Celtic Tiger narrative was widely accepted in the profession.

As it happened, Rabbitte and O'Keeffe were correct to articulate the fears of workers, which turned out to be all too well founded. The problem was that they and their colleagues took fright at the dressing down and never mentioned it again. Unfortunately, the political establishment were taking their orders from the media, instead of fearlessly pursuing the interests of the Irish people, even if that involved taking a stand on the migration issue, which was soon to play such a crucial role in creating and compounding our economic woes.

The Road to Ruin

The serious lack of moral fibre on the part of politicians in capitulating to the self-righteousness of the media, an inability to take hard decisions and the Irish need to win every popularity contest, brought us to the brink of economic catastrophe and very nearly bankrupted the country. The major elements of the crash were all linked in one way or another to immigration. The housing bubble was the result of the enormous demand that suddenly arose when large-scale inward migration took off. The toxic consensus that supported and encouraged the Celtic Tiger boom and the mass migration episode that accompanied it, were never questioned by those whose business it was to do so. The banking crisis was a direct result of the property price collapse, over-borrowing and the failure of the regulatory agencies to take the hard decisions required to restore order. When migration got out of control after the EU enlargement, the government and the unions should have had the gumption to close the unfettered access door, even if it involved losing the EU Commission's best small European country contest. When mass unemployment almost sank the economy in 2009, we should have had the moral fibre to invoke the clause that the Spaniards used in 2011, when they refused entry to Romanians because of distortion of their labour market. In the aftermath of the crash, the government and the Department of Education should have used the opportunity and bestirred themselves to challenge the academic establishment and radically reform the third level sector with a view to matching apprentice, technician and graduate output with the requirements of the economy and society, rather than importing key workers. We did none of these things, in part because our leaders and those who influence public opinion, could not countenance advocating anything that might in any way be construed as being politically incorrect. This ruled out drawing any conclusions about our troubles that had any linkage, however remote, to the elephant in the room, immigration.

6

The Welfare State

The fall of the Celtic Tiger had enormous repercussions for Irish society and the economy. Repercussions that were widespread but were most keenly felt by the 300,000 private sector workers, mainly at the lower end of the labour market, who lost their jobs and the tens of thousands who were forced or decided, to emigrate – 46,500 Irish nationals in 2012 alone. Because of who they were and the relatively low profile of their contribution to the economy, it is easy to forget the losses they suffered and the price they paid for the debacle. Close to half a million workers, out of a two million workforce (see Fig. 5-2), were unemployed for up to six years after the 2008 Crash. Many of them and their families became dependant on the welfare state.

While it is almost inevitable that people will endure at least one or two periods of unemployment in a lifetime's work, the safety net of the welfare state is there to assist in these circumstances. This safety net does not come cheap. It is normally paid for by the social insurance contributions of employees and employers while at work. This is the understanding at the very heart of the social contract underpinning the welfare state. The situation of the recently arrived migrant is not the same as the lifetime contributor, as many may have only a relatively short period of work in the host country and consequently have not built up the same level of entitlement, in terms of payments into the welfare fund. The system works because pay-outs and contributions balance out over time. Whether it is fully justified or not, the spectacle of large numbers of migrants crowding into social welfare offices all over the country, expecting and getting the same level of support as people who had worked hard and contributed all their lives, undermined the social solidarity and sense of fairness essential to the functioning of the welfare state. Many of the large numbers of immigrants on social welfare, who arrived just before and after the crash, never contributed anything at all to the social welfare kitty. For the beneficiaries of the Celtic Tiger business boom and their supporters, this was of little importance but not so for the silent taxpaying public.

Large-scale inward migration is a direct challenge to the understanding that underpins the welfare state. The welfare state exists because workers agree to pay hefty social security taxes when they are in a position to do so and draw benefits when they need them. When large-scale immigration takes place, the host country and its taxpayers must either foot the bill for the benefits which the new arrivals can then enjoy, or attempt to restrict them. When the British allowed unfettered access to their labour market on the accession of the ten new EU members in 2004, they attempted to restrict access to the benefits of their welfare state. They did not succeed.

In a radio interview at the time, Tony Blair said *'if they can't support themselves they will be put out of the country* '[1], a typical piece of political bluster for public consumption, that could not be delivered upon. The European Commission quickly responded through Antonia Mochan, spokeswoman for the Commissioner for Employment and Social Affairs, who said *'as far as social security is concerned the principle of non-discrimination between nationals of old and new member states applies from 1st May'* (2004). In allowing unfettered access to our labour markets, both the British and the Irish Governments were also allowing unfettered access to the benefits of our welfare states.

At a time of relatively full employment this was not much of a concern, in Ireland at least. Not noted for forward thinking, the Irish Government carried on as if the Celtic Tiger boom would never end. But before long, it did, and with a vengeance. The undertakings of the welfare state were then called upon in very substantial measure, not just by those who had paid for them, but also by those who had just recently arrived.

When the Tide Turned

When large numbers of people first arrive in a country looking for work, many of them are likely to end up at the bottom of the pile and will struggle, at least initially, to make ends meet. This may involve them being dependent on the state, either totally through the social welfare system or partially through other state-funded assistance programmes, for varying periods of time.

The newly arrived will not have paid anything into the kitty or if they have, it will have been for a relatively short time compared to native labour. At the time of the crash in 2008 less than 70,000 of the Celtic Tiger migrant influx had been here for ten years or more and less than half had been here for four years. How many of these had been economically active and paying social security contributions is anybody's guess.

It takes a significant time to build up the resources required to fund even a short period of dependency. For migrants arriving in a high cost country like Ireland, with a few weeks' expenses in their back pockets, a surprising number did find work in the Celtic Tiger period. However, when the tide turned in the middle of 2007 and the economy stagnated, the work soon dried up. The problem for Ireland and its welfare state was that the flood of migrants continued and those already here who lost their jobs mostly stayed put. Large numbers ended up on the dole queues, drawing social welfare from a fund to which they had not contributed sufficiently, if at all.

As the stagnation of 2007 and early 2008 turned into the catastrophe of late 2008 the flood of migration proceeded unabated. Over those two years a net figure of 141,000 people came to live and 'work' in Ireland. What is certain is that only a very small proportion of those people found work. A number were dependants but the rest signed on the dole, to what they must have thought was a gravy train compared to what they would get at home. Many of their compatriots who had come here earlier and found work would also become clients of the welfare state.

For the native population who had largely paid for these benefits and were now having to call on them themselves, this was a hard pill to swallow. If they had realised the full extent to which they were being taken advantage of, their resentment might have been much greater. The media however, kept information, comment and discussion to a bare minimum on this aspect of welfare funding and the political pressure to address the situation never developed to the point where something might have been done.

Meanwhile the Great Recession took hold and the dole queues lengthened at an alarming rate, making the undertakings of the welfare state even more onerous. By the spring of 2010, a bare eighteen months into the recession, there were 432,000 on the live register and another 60,000 on job schemes, making a grand total of almost half a million people out of work. In this situation, it might reasonably be expected that substantial numbers of migrants would return home. This did not happen. For almost every one that did leave, a replacement arrived, so that at the end of the recession the migrant population was still more or less the same as it had been at the beginning.

The Celtic Gravy Train

There was of course, a good reason for this. The Irish welfare state, for a minimal contribution had provided a generous array of benefits to a large part of its migrant population for the duration of the crisis, paid out of the general fund supplied by the Irish Exchequer. Some of the money had come from the taxpayers' social insurance contributions, but because of the large numbers involved, recourse had to be made to borrowings on the financial markets. Notwithstanding, the desired result was achieved and we kept our guests in the comfort, albeit frugal by some standards, to which they had become accustomed and which was obviously a lot better than they could have done at home.

After the crash of 2008, and even for a short period before, Ireland ceased to be a place where work was available. Yet the attraction in the minds of migrants persisted right through the recession. In the likely event of their not finding work, a reasonably good living could be had on the benefits of the Irish welfare state. Irish benefits were a good deal better than in the United Kingdom, with the main 'Jobseekers benefit' being twice the rate of its UK equivalent. Most of our migrants were coming from Eastern Europe, where Irish unemployment benefits were considerably better than paid employment in their home countries. These could then be supplemented with a whole range of other benefits which our welfare officials seemed to be more than happy to give. So happy in fact, that they produced booklets in their native languages on how to make claims, as well as providing form-filling assistance.

The enthusiasm on behalf of government and public officials to shovel out money, paid in, largely by the native workforce or borrowed, on foot of claims on the welfare state was in sharp contrast to the perception that the economy was on its knees. Even though government revenue had plummeted by €12 billion (23 per cent) between 2007 and 2009, expenditure on social welfare had risen by €5 billion in the same period to an annual €20.5 billion. This became necessary because of the huge rise in unemployment, compounded by the continuing inward migration after the crash. Working Age Income Supports more than doubled from €2.8 billion in 2005 to €6.3 billion in 2009. Illness, Disability and Carers allowances almost doubled from €2.1 billion in 2005 to €3.5 billion in 2009, which, in itself, is a strange story that has never been examined or explained. Did the economic crash trigger a wave of ill-health? Even Children's Allowances rose from €2.0 billion in 2005 to €2.8 billion in 2009, indicating a population explosion coincident with the crash, which subsequently fell back to €2.3 billion in 2014.

The funding for the social protection aspect of government was by far the single biggest expenditure, at nearly one third of all public spending. Despite the meltdown in the public finances after the crash, the government must be given full credit for having maintained, almost intact, the undertakings of the welfare state, in value and scope terms. This was a significant achievement, secured most probably against much pressure from the global financial establishment and the European political elite, who would have had no compunction in reducing welfare payments to a minimum, as they forced the Greeks to do. That being said, it would have been much less expensive, if the immigrant cohort had reduced significantly, as would have happened elsewhere.

The price to be paid for holding the line on social welfare added significantly to our enormous national debt. One has to wonder if maintaining the real value of social welfare payments had anything to do with the steely insistence by the ECB that all bondholders, whether secured or not, had to be paid in full. The money to bridge the gap between government income and expenditure had to be borrowed and now forms a substantial part of our €200 billion national debt, or around €100,000 for every worker in the state.

Almost 1.8 million people were receiving a weekly social welfare payment in 2008. By 2012 that figure had grown to 2.259 million out of a population of 4.6m or nearly one out of every two people. Government expenditure on social welfare was €20.8 billion in 2012 or almost 31 per cent of the national budget. For the bottom half of Irish society, the redistribution of wealth carried out by the welfare state through the social welfare system is vital to their wellbeing. It is also vital to the social cohesion of the state.

If the present level of inward migration continues and another economic crash of similar proportions were to occur, it is doubtful if the generous Irish welfare state could be maintained in its present form or even survive at all. The financial overhang of the national debt and the interest payments required to service it would probably take precedence over another substantial call on resources to support our welfare system. On the last occasion (2008) a reasonable reserve had been built up, in contrast to today, where, in place of a modest reserve there is a mountain of debt. The policy of allowing huge numbers of migrants into the state, many of whom would become welfare dependants particularly in an economic downturn, is reckless in the extreme. But this is exactly what we are currently doing. Over the last four years a net 116,800 (CSO) non-nationals have arrived here to take up residence and work, or almost 600 a week. Meanwhile, there are still substantial numbers on the dole (200,000 on the live register including part-timers and 50,000 on 'activation' schemes in January 2019), who should be filling any vacancies that occur and saving on welfare payments at the same time.

The Welfare Tourist

The Irish experience of immigration since the crash, confirms a truth that was there for all to see but was too politically incorrect to be mentioned. The phenomenon of the welfare tourist came to its full flowering in the aftermath of the crash. The furthest extremity of the phenomenon was the case of 600 'welfare tourists' – they were literally tourists – uncovered by the Department of Social Protection, living abroad and travelling to Ireland regularly, to collect payments (article in the *Sunday Times* 18 December 2011)[2]. This investigation saved the tax-payer €6.3 million.

However, a much more serious manifestation of the problem was the enormous numbers that continued to arrive throughout the recession. While the Irish economy was on its knees, with in excess of 400,000 unemployed in the seven year period from 2009 to 2015, a total of 287,600 non-national migrants arrived on our shores (CSO), to live and presumably work here. Almost every individual who departed was replaced by a new arrival in a country racked by unemployment. What were they doing here? Were they all computer programmers, medical specialists or engineers with advanced skills that couldn't be found in Ireland? Were they the leading-edge individuals required by our multi-national companies who couldn't be found here – 118,300 of them had to be issued with work-permits because they were not even EU citizens? This is very hard to believe. One would have thought that it would have been reasonable to expect that far fewer would arrive and a far greater number would leave, to pursue their ambitions elsewhere, but this never happened. At the end of the period we had less than 10,000 fewer migrants. The only conclusion that can be drawn is that, for many, the prospect of life on benefits here had its attractions.

A large number of the migrant cohort that arrived here in the aftermath of the crash, were not innocents on some wild-goose chase seeking non-existent work. Of the immigrants that came here between 2006 and 2011, only one out of seven ended up in employment[3]. Perhaps they were not looking for work, which begs the question why were they here. The welfare tourist, was and still is, a widespread and flourishing species in Ireland.

Obvious, as the abuse of taxpayers' money is, any attempt to quantify the cost is invariably dismissed as anti-migrant sentiment. This is part of a general reluctance to forensically and critically investigate and evaluate the benefits of large-scale inward migration to Irish society as a whole and not just to the business sector. It's the Irish version of what might be called 'the Rotherham Syndrome' in Britain, where criminality, illegal activities, scams and fraud engaged in by migrants or refugees were tolerated, due to an oversensitivity about allocating blame when race is a factor in the situation. This is a widespread phenomenon in Western Europe and here in Ireland.

A number of independent, professional and rigorously unbiased studies should be undertaken into exactly how migration impacted on the operation of our welfare state, the native unemployed, the public finances and the property sector. The public are entitled to know how many people came here and never worked at all or had minimal work activity. Studies should also investigate why the educational establishment is not providing a suitable range of training and educational options to match our unemployed and indeed our school-leavers to the opportunities which are now filled by immigrants.

Send us your Huddled Masses

The lack of data and transparency and the partisan agendas of interest groups with ready access to an uncritical media, make it difficult to investigate the cost or otherwise of migration to Irish society and in particular the effect it is having on the bottom half of society which is impacted most. Undoubtedly migrants who work contribute greatly to the profitability of the enterprises where they are employed and thereby benefit their owners and the Irish exchequer through their taxes. However, the numbers at work and the duration of their employment are difficult to decipher from the data available. An article in the *Sunday Times* 4 September 2011[4] says, in a comment about our ability to monitor and manage our social welfare system: *'The minister (Joan Burton at the time) has no database that tells her how much each individual or household is getting. This is hardly a surprise, her department is running a system in which 7.2m PPS numbers are extant in a country with a registered population of 4.6m'*. A large number of these PPS numbers were issued to migrants who came here in the last twenty years. Immigrants in other countries are required to register their address with the authorities, so that they know who is in the country at any time. This should also be the case here, where there is a large transient population, some of whom might be tempted to make fraudulent claims. Information on the nature and duration of migrant claims on the social welfare system are not clear from the available data.

All migrant children, pensioners and unemployed would have been entitled to welfare payments. For those who were working, particularly in low paid jobs as many migrants were, there was a range of other welfare 'supplementary' payments available such as family income supplement and miscellaneous payments and grants, all paid for by the taxpayer. While living costs were much higher here, wages were generally three to four times those of the accession states (to the EU) and the minimum wage legislation drew a base line below which most legitimate businesses did not go. Higher wages enabled migrants to pay higher rents and in the last resort the state would step in and supplement housing costs if that became necessary. The building boom was producing nearly 90,000 residential units a year at its height, so there was no shortage of accommodation, at a price of course. Another box was ticked in the migration incentive form.

An example of how the social welfare system works in relation to migration can be gleaned from the CSO Employment and Social Welfare activity of foreign nationals data. In 2008 a total of

154,788 PPS numbers were issued to foreign nationals, 27,068 were to under 15s, 2372 were to over 65s and 53,421 of the rest had no employment at any point in the following three years. Of the remaining 74,289, a figure of 61,758 (40 per cent of the total 2008 arrival number) were listed as having employment activity, but by 2011 this employment activity figure had halved to 30,521 (20 per cent). Employment activity is defined by the CSO, in this instance, as meaning employment that 'can vary from having worked one day in the year to working full-time throughout the year'. This definition of 'employment activity' is not much use in determining economic activity. So, of those that came in 2008, one in five of the arrivals was working at some level three years later and undoubtedly some of them had gone home.

When commentators extol the benefits of migration, often with great conviction, where is the hard evidence of benefit to the host community? The above example is very short on any indication that a great amount of economic activity was contributed by the migrant cohort of 2008. The impression indicated by the figures, is that there was a high rate of dependency on state benefits by this group of migrants, with only 20 per cent engaging in any employment activity three years later. Far better methods and measurements are required before credible claims regarding the benefits of migration can be made.

Child Welfare

Back in 2003, the then Minister for Justice Michael McDowell was reported as claiming that up to half of all non-EU mothers who gave birth to children in this country, did so to obtain citizenship for the child. He was immediately challenged on the grounds that it was impossible for him to work out the motives of those concerned. But before long the general thrust of the claim seemed to be vindicated. *The Irish Times* of 20 November 2013[5], reporting about the birth rate in Ireland and inward migration said *'In that year (2004) a total of 18 per cent of births were to mothers from outside Ireland. That figure reached 25 per cent in 2011 and remained unchanged last year'*(2012). With the growing adult migrant population since then, it is probable that the 25 per cent share of births to migrant mothers has now been exceeded by some distance. It is indeed astonishing to think that more than one quarter of children attending our schools and crèches have a least one foreign parent. This remarkable statistic can leave us in no doubt as to the depth of the fundamental demographic transformation that has been taking place in Ireland.

Despite the huge costs involved, in both education (€11.19 billion in 2020) and child welfare (€2.88 billion in 2020), the Irish welfare state provides a wide range of assistance and support to the children who reside here, regardless of nationality. The main support is a tax-free monthly child benefit payment of €140/month for each child (it was €166/month in 2008). It is one of the most generous support schemes of its kind in Europe and may well have provided at least part of the incentive to place Ireland at the top of the birth-rate league in the EU. No doubt it was another encouragement, if one was needed, for migrating parents to head for the emerald isle. The Irish Children's Allowance (child benefit) is a little less than a sixth of the average net wage in Poland (in 2016). The equivalent child benefit in Poland is €21/month, in Lithuania it is €15.2/month, in Latvia it is €11.38/month[6] and in non-EU countries it's probably a whole lot less. The Irish child benefit is being paid to almost 8,000 children who still reside in their home countries but have a parent working here, which is generosity above and beyond the call of duty.

There are a wide range of child-related benefit entitlements in Ireland including an Affordable Childcare Scheme which is worth €1,000 annually for each child, enhanced for those on lower incomes, to assist in childcare costs for the under 6s. A Qualified

Child Payment of €36/week is paid to parents on social welfare and a Back to School Clothing and Footwear Allowance of between €150 to €275 a year can be claimed by those who qualify, to defray school attendance expenses. There is also a school meals programme which cost €35 million (in 2012). For the vast majority of migrants who were from Eastern Europe and poorer third countries, these benefits were extremely generous when compared to equivalent benefits in their homelands. They provided yet another strongly positive incentive to pack their bags and make the move to Ireland.

Education

The large-scale migration to Ireland that has taken place in the last twenty five years means that the educational requirements of a large number of child migrants must now be catered for by the Irish state. As referred to earlier, in 2008 alone 27,000 PPS numbers were issued to such children under 15 and almost 55,000 to the 15 to 24 year age group, many of whom would also be using the educational facilities of the state at secondary and third level. These facilities come at a considerable cost to the taxpayer. In fact, Education and Skills is the third most expensive government department, which will cost €11.2 billion in 2020.

Special facilities are often required for migrant children who cannot speak English, which involve extra cost to the schools they attend and ultimately to the taxpayer. The 2016 Census reveals that 612,000 people in Ireland speak a foreign language at home and 184,000 of these were born here. Most of the latter, are presumably the children of immigrants. The educational experience of indigenous pupils, in some cases, may be compromised by the extra effort required to assist those with communication difficulties, for whom English is not their first language. It is a tribute to the staff of schools that these difficulties have not caused more disruption.

An extraordinary fact emerged, in the course of a discussion recently on a television programme (RTE Prime Time 28th January 2020), when resourcing education was being talked about. A school-principal in a small town in the West of Ireland complained that she needed extra resources to cope with a situation where 40 per cent of her pupils did not understand or needed help understanding English – presumably they were the children of immigrants. Nobody batted an eyelid at this revelation and there appeared to be a general acceptance in the group that the government – the taxpayer – should step up to the plate forthwith and provide the required funding.

With at least a quarter of children in the state born to women who were born outside Ireland and many more coming here with migrating parents, the extra burden on the taxpayer in relation to education is very considerable. While acknowledging that working migrants are contributing to the cost of the service, the educational establishment we have today is the result of more than one hundred years of investment, in good times and bad. The increased burden of providing educational facilities for large numbers of migrant children, while undoubtedly beneficial for them, is another reason to challenge the conventional view that migration is always beneficial to the host society.

The Health Service

An opinion poll published on 10 September 2008[(7)] indicated that 72 per cent of those asked were 'a little worried' or 'extremely worried' about the health service in relation to migration. Eleven years later and with an extra 0.5 million or more clients, many of them immigrants, it can be said with some certainty that their fears were well founded. The health service has struggled to provide a satisfactory service to the public in recent years. Long waiting lists for public patients – over 780,000 according to a report on RTE on 15th October 2019 – have damaged its reputation and a lack of resources and staff in accident and emergency departments has undermined public confidence in the service.

The requirement to cut costs in the aftermath of the crash and an embargo on recruitment, together with a perception of poor and top heavy management, were all part of a number of problems that beset the service. The key factor however, was more than likely the surge in immigration that accompanied the Celtic Tiger period and still continues today, which helped push the population up by more than a million. This stretched the health service to its limits as the resources available made it difficult to cater for the increased demand.

This overstretched health service is now unable to provide timely treatment and diagnostic appointments to more than half the residents of the state that depend on it and who, through their social insurance contributions have paid for it. Hospital bed availability is poor and overcrowding in accident and emergency departments is chronic. The per capita hospital bed ratio and the number of general practitioners per head of population is below that of most developed countries. The Irish health service is in a very fragile state and will find it difficult to respond adequately to any health emergency, due to the rapid increase in population.

The health service is an extremely large, complex and expensive institution to run. Like other public institutions it is not something that was created overnight, but is the result of the efforts of dedicated staff who work there now and in the past and of generations of workers who paid for it. The cost of providing this service was over €13 billion in 2016 and is growing at an alarming rate – it is estimated to cost €18.33 billion in 2020, 30 per cent more than it was four years ago – while the service it is providing is deteriorating as it becomes more overstretched. It is the second most expensive item in government expenditure.

The Welfare State in Jeopardy

The conventional view, widely held in the media, business, and politics and by the 'progressive' tendency in society, is that migration is a good thing and perhaps from their perspective it is. For the rest of us this is not necessarily the case. The addition of almost one million people from elsewhere, to the Irish population in the last twenty five years had enormous benefits for the business community in terms of lower labour costs and increased demand for housing, goods and services. The commercial opportunities offered by the relatively sudden expansion of the population were vast for those in a position to take advantage of them. However, when the tide turned and the economy crashed, the ones to suffer most were the bottom half of the indigenous population. The tab for this monumental disaster has not or will not be picked up by the business elite, the new landlord class, the bankers, the speculators or any of the beneficiaries of the Celtic Tiger episode. The bill is being paid and will continue to be paid by the workers of this country and their children.

Should another similar episode occur – and with the cyclical nature of market economics and the current political and financial instability, the question is not if but when – the consequences could be a lot worse than those we experienced after 2008. Even if the national debt were to remain static but interest rates were to move off the historic lows of the present, the cost of servicing the debt – estimated at €6 to 7 billion in recent years – could increase significantly. The chances of an Irish Government debt default could loom large if expenditure got out of control as it did in 2008. There is no doubt that in such circumstances the benefits of the welfare state would be significantly unwound. Ireland could experience a downward economic and social spiral similar to what has happened in Greece.

If the Irish welfare state is to be preserved, maintained and defended, it cannot endure another haemorrhage like the recession of 2008 to 2015 when it had to be propped up by borrowings. The free market exuberance and the hyper expansion of the Celtic Tiger period must be curbed and replaced by sustainable economic activity which delivers jobs, prosperity and security to our own people. Allowing another flood of migration to create and then exaggerate the boom and bust economic cycle of that era is a recipe for chaos, dysfunctionality and disaster. It may benefit the short-term self-serving interests of powerful groups but ultimately it is an attack on the common good.

Back in 2008 and indeed long before, the general public were opposed to the high levels of migration into Ireland and rightly fearful of the consequences of the continuing influx. The concerns of the public, then and now are being ignored. Migration into Ireland is beginning to accelerate rapidly again. There is no doubt that the public will not be consulted about migration policy unless they insist on voicing their opinions in a much more effective way than heretofore. A great debate, like the one that is taking place all over Europe on every television news channel every night, must begin in Ireland. Otherwise the powerful groups who dictate economic policy, the political establishment and the liberal elite who share many of their views, will continue to ignore the concerns of the public on this fundamental issue.

7

The Property Bubble

The Irish love affair with property is legendary. It probably goes back at least to the pre-Famine era in the nineteenth century when Irish peasants rented tiny plots of land from rack-renting landlords who could evict them at will. The Famine and its aftermath saw a biblical land clearance which today would probably be described as an ethnic cleansing episode. It was an event of immense significance that may well have left a deep scar on the Irish psyche.

The hunger for secure tenure was − and still is − a powerful force in Irish society. The Bull McCabe's obsession with the patch of land portrayed in *The Field* still strongly resonates in the Irish soul. It has left the Irish vulnerable to the pitfalls of greed and covetousness where property is concerned. The ocean of credit that beckoned in the late 1990s seduced many an unwary soul into indulging their property passions, without due regard to the risks involved.

It was not just the passion for property and the need for security that drove the Celtic Tiger property bubble. Like their predecessors in the post-Famine era who quickly gobbled up the possessions of the starving, fleeing masses and the dead, the motivation for much of what went on in the Celtic Tiger period had a strong element of opportunistic greed. The notion of playing the nineteenth-century landlord at his own game had widespread appeal and there was no shortage of tenants to exploit in the newly arrived army of migrants. With a banking sector eager to facilitate the ambitions of a new gombeen class, the stage was set for a property orgy.

The Property Bandwagon

An enormous number of houses and apartments were built in the nine-year period from 2000 to 2008. Almost three times the normal domestic requirement of between 20,000 and 25,000 units a year were built. In total, more than 600,000 or a yearly average of almost 68,000 were built in that period according to official statistics. At the height of the building boom in 2006 over 93,400 dwellings were completed and more than 275,000 well paid construction workers were employed in the sector.

Property Bubble House Completions

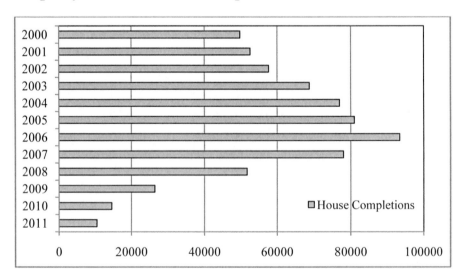

Fig. 7-1 Department of Finance figures for house completions in the Celtic Tiger period and after the crash. The CSO in the 2016 Census notes a mere 8,800 increase in the housing stock since the 2011 Census, a tiny figure for a five-year period. Total house completions in the five year period were 33,436.

The price of property became a national obsession in the Celtic Tiger period. Soaring house price inflation, according to NCB Stockbrokers in a study that featured in an article in the *Irish Independent* on 29th November 2005[(1)] was, would you believe, *'helping borrowers'*. They quoted an example of a 90 per cent mortgage taken out to buy an average house in 2003. Two years later this would stand at just 67 per cent of the value of the house. With no effort involved, a huge capital gain could be made. The reason advanced by NCB, for the 'buoyant' house prices, was simple. They contended, and here they were undoubtedly correct, that *'the arrival of 11,000 migrant workers a month will keep demand for new houses at record levels'*. Not only that, but they confidently predicted that *'the house market will be buoyant for the next fifteen years'*, at 75,000 units a year! It highlighted *'immigration as the key to sustaining the current pace of house completions'*. NCB believed that *'immigration is likely to accelerate because of the freedom of access granted to citizens of the ten new EU countries'*. There was encouragement in the report for the faint-hearted who had yet to jump on the property band-wagon. It said *'the rise in debt in Ireland is not a problem because of borrowers' ability to pay'*. A long road of prosperity stretched out before us, thanks to large-scale migration from Eastern Europe and beyond and the intense demand for accommodation that it created. **(See Appendix 6 for the full text of the article)**

NCB's figures were borne out by the Department of Finance's monthly report where they told us that the average new house cost €225,000 in 2003 and the price in 2005 was €275,000 − 22 per cent more. Another Department of Finance report (on page 9) in September 2008 carried a graph showing new house price inflation averaging 11% for the 7 year period from 2000 to 2006 and 12.5% for second hand houses. The implication of the NCB study seemed to be that the value of property assets is appreciating at a phenomenal rate, so get on the bandwagon before it's too late.

A couple of months later, another glowing forecast was published. Irish Intercontinental Bank (IIB) senior economist Austin Hughes – and he was considered a conservative forecaster – was quoted at length in the *Irish Independent* on 25 January 2006[2]. Announcing his 2006 forecast for the property market. He predicted that *'a new wave of immigration will help drive property price growth of 8% this year'* (2006). He said *'the number of migrant workers here already "dwarfs" UK levels'*. He talked, with great enthusiasm, about the 137,000 Poles who came in 2005 and said that *'this extraordinary number may well be just the first wave'*. Later in the article he signalled that the chances of the 'bubble bursting' were remote. There was a reference to fast rising private sector debt levels of €260 billion which raised fears that debt was spiralling out of control. Mr Hughes played down these fears insisting that Irish consumers were in fact *'under-borrowed'*. In his very obviously upbeat feeling about the market, he noted that householders had €545 billion worth of positive equity in their homes. In hindsight, it was equity that quickly evaporated after the crash. But he was undoubtedly right about one thing and that was the key role played by mass migration in creating huge demand for property.

Mr Hughes was not alone in his enthusiasm. Bank of Ireland's Dan McLaughlin added his voice to the chorus cheering on the Celtic Tiger. In his forecast for 2006[3] he predicted that mortgage debt of €97.5 billion would grow by another €21 billion with the construction of 75,000 new houses. As late as 19 December 2006 the *Irish Independent*[4] reported that Goodbody Stockbrokers predicted economic growth of 5.6 per cent in 2007 due to the surge in immigrants from Eastern Europe which had boosted both the supply and demand sides of the economy. With the encouragement of these eminent people and an unfailingly positive spin from the media, all and sundry, big and small tried to elbow their way to the trough. The party went on for another year and then, as we all now know, it came to a shuddering stop.

Panic, to get on the property ladder before they were priced out of the market and greed, combined in an unholy union. Egged on by the financial sector and their experts and the media, which had been gripped by a bout of the same 'irrational exuberance' that had been experienced in the United States earlier, the property orgy became a frenzy. By 2007 the average new house cost €322,624 nationwide, while in Dublin it was €416,225 (according to the Department of Finance report and the Housing Statistics Workbook September 2008). Normal rules did not seem to apply, such was the intensity of the forces driving the market. Despite the 78,027 new house completions in 2007, three times the normal requirement, the thirst for property could not be slaked.

That was the toxic consensus that held sway at the height of the Celtic Tiger period. The hundreds of thousands of migrants who had arrived on our shores in the previous ten years had to be housed or otherwise they would have had to sleep on the streets. The answer was simple, accommodation would have to be found for them. Few of them bought houses themselves – they couldn't afford to – so they usually rented. This opened up a marvellous commercial opportunity for the middle classes with a bit of spare money to invest. The bricks and mortar option was secure, almost risk-free, paid a handsome return and at the same time was doing a necessary good in sheltering the weary migrant. It was almost a Good Samaritan moment, with the added advantage of income generation from an appreciating capital asset. Not only that, but valuable tax incentives were also available to those participating, whereby costs incurred could be written off against tax due on the income generated.

The investing classes were not found wanting. They swarmed into the housing market with great enthusiasm, pushing prices to unsustainable heights. Buyers looking for a place to live were panicked into paying exorbitant prices or pushed out of the way. The tax incentives to the landlords and the cheap money fanned the flames of an already overheated market. The bubble waxed large.

Many of the new builds were bought by investors with a view to getting into the rental market. With up to half a million migrants and many Irish who could not afford to buy, looking to rent, there was no shortage of clients. The 2011 Census reports that there were 474,788 rented dwellings in the state (about one quarter of the total number of dwellings), up a staggering 47 per cent on the 2006 Census. This indicated a sea change in how Irish people would live their lives in the future and it would be a change for the worse. The legitimate ambition of home ownership for all was beginning to crumble. The notion that ordinary people with jobs could be priced out of the market had become a reality. Even though three times the normal number of houses required per annum in Ireland were being built, people could not afford to buy. This did not bode well for a time of short supply.

Meanwhile the extra numbers forced into the rental market pushed up rents. The average weekly rent in Dun Laoghaire-Rathdown was €275 in 2006 or more than €1,000 a month. Extra pressure in the rental sector was added to by migrants from the accession states who usually rented, which is probably what they did in their home countries. The 2011 census confirmed this, informing us that only 4,500 mortgages were held by this group (Census 2011 Results)[5].

The Bubble Bursts

By 2007 we had reached the top of the hill as far as property was concerned. What we failed to realise was that just below the crest of the hill on the other side, was a cliff. When we went headlong over it in September 2008 we were vainly hoping for a soft landing. The sub-prime crisis in the United States and the global financial meltdown that followed ensured we had a very hard landing.

The property bubble had overloaded the financial sector with toxic debt while the regulatory authorities were asleep. The government had stoked the flames of irrationality with ill-considered tax breaks. The media and the financial and economic establishment had promised a decade-and-a-half of full-on growth, fuelled by mass migration. Hubris and greed convinced the investing class to shed their inhibitions about prudence and risk and go for broke on property.

When the crunch came, many of the buy-to-let as well as the buy-to-live found their incomes shrinking. The 180,000 job losses that occurred within a year of the crash, along with falling or stagnant income took their toll on their ability to pay. One third of mortgages were in negative equity by 2010. House prices were down 50 per cent and apartments were 60 per cent lower by 2012, from the 2007 peak. Following the crash almost a quarter of Irish mortgages were in arrears or had been restructured. The value of buy-to-let mortgage accounts in arrears was €8.7 billion by mid-2013.

The destabilisation of the financial sector caused by the collapse of the property bubble was an unmitigated disaster for the Irish economy and for many of the individuals caught up in it. It also cost the workers of this country dearly because it was socialised by the government's actions and foisted onto the public. As usual, the bill for this debacle did not fall on the culprits, the property speculators or the bankers who lent them the money. The hefty

€62.8 billion bill for stabilising the financial sector was picked up by the Irish taxpayer. Several hundred thousand people who bought properties to live in now found themselves trapped in a negative equity situation and were paying off enormous loans for properties worth half what they had paid for them. Many of the speculators who drove up prices in the first place continued to rent and use their tax breaks. Central to their welfare was the ability of the migrant population to pay, which they did, albeit often with taxpayer's money in the form of rental supplements from social welfare.

The most important underlying factor in the surge of property speculation that took place in Ireland in the Celtic Tiger period was the sudden expansion of demand. Without turbocharged demand, prices might have remained relatively stable. Instead, between 1996 and 2011 the population suddenly increased by almost one million or 27 per cent, creating huge demand for housing. This single fact emboldened speculators and convinced financial institutions of the merits of construction projects all over the country. The NCB report quoted earlier, where they identified mass migration as the key to sustaining the construction of 75,000 houses a year – for the following fifteen years to 2020 – was typical of the rationale that drove the great Irish property splurge.

This obviously was a view that was widely held in banking circles at the time, hence the extraordinary volume of lending that took place and the ferocious competition between the lending institutions. Not only were the Irish financial institutions convinced that this could continue but so were the major European banks that lent them at least €100 billion, the money that ultimately financed these operations.

The key role of mass migration in underpinning property prices was not just a view held by a select few at the top of the financial institutions. Many of the punters in the buy-to-let business were keenly aware of who was providing them with handsome returns on their investments. They and indeed some of the more market orientated general population of house owners, were well aware of the competitive forces at work, relentlessly pushing up house prices. No other asset class in Ireland at the time could produce the same return on capital as residential property.

With the near collapse of the banks in 2008 came a liquidity crisis that virtually halted all lending and sent the construction sector into meltdown and house prices through the floor. House completions dropped like a stone, from 78,027 in 2007, to 51,724 in 2008, to 26,420 in 2009, to 14,602 in 2010.

Individual migrants themselves, no less than the native population, were victims of the rocketing costs of housing in the Celtic Tiger period. The demand, which underpinned the market, was identified time and again by the leading financial and economic analysts, as the prolonged mass immigration episode. Very high levels of inward migration today continue to fuel rocketing rents as demand tightens and supply falters. The beneficiaries were and still are the landlords who collect their steadily rising rents, many of which are subsidised by the taxpayer.

The Current Housing Crisis

Meanwhile, the housing problem has now become one of chronic under supply, particularly in the Dublin area where it has become acute. House completions for the five year period from 2011 to 2016 were just 33,436 according to the CSO or less than 6,700 per year when the requirement is nearer to 25,000. The number of occupied dwellings was virtually the same in 2011 as it was in 2016 at 1.7 million although the population had risen by 173,000. Since then the population has risen by another 159,000 and the construction industry is struggling to build 20,000 houses per year. A substantial backlog of at least 100,000 houses has built up over the last seven years due to the lack of building activity since the crash. Homelessness and a chronic housing shortage, coupled with unsustainable rent and house price rises has become a major problem.

The liquidity crisis in the banks was partially responsible for the lack of building activity after the crash, which in turn has resulted in a very meagre supply of houses for sale. This has forced prices up to the level of the pre-crash Celtic Tiger days in Dublin. These high prices have side-lined many potential buyers and forced them into the social and affordable category where they must rely on the state or voluntary sector to provide them with housing.

Many of these first-time buyers, who would have bought at the lower end of the market, have been forced into the rental sector, which is already overcrowded, to the extent that rents are rising even faster than house prices. The strict Central Bank of Ireland rules on lending, which require house purchasers to have a substantial deposit, is adding to the difficulties of young people caught in the double bind of trying to save, while paying very high rents. All these factors are combining to deny people on modest incomes, the possibility of ever owning their own homes.

The government has failed to control rents or increase the housing supply sufficiently, which is hardly surprising, when 26.5 per cent of the members of Dail Eireann (in 2019) were landlords[6]. Irish governments seldom interfere with market mechanisms because they are usually dancing to the tune of some vested interest that is calling the shots – in this case the landlord lobby, of which they themselves are enthusiastic members. Large build-to-rent investors are now major players in the Irish property market. They owned 12,000 properties at the end of June 2019, mainly in the Dublin area, with many more in the pipeline. Other so called 'vulture funds' are also substantial players in the Irish property market, having been sold huge tranches of taxpayer-owned property by NAMA, for what some would say were knock-down prices .

In a situation where demand outstrips supply by a wide margin, as in today's housing market, the buyer and the tenant suffer. If the supply of 20-25,000 housing units satisfies the market, then the annual number of new occupiers should be around 50,000 people. A key factor, that is seldom if ever mentioned when the housing crisis is discussed in Ireland, is the number of migrants who arrive in the country each year and who obviously must be housed.

The curious dynamics of the Irish property market are needless to say, difficult to understand. When the market was in oversupply in the Celtic Tiger period, demand soared and prices rocketed, fuelled by fear and greed. Undersupply is now also pushing prices up, this time in a more logical response, that is likely to continue until supply and demand achieve a balance. In the meantime, and into the foreseeable future, the people who will suffer most are likely to be young indigenous Irish workers on modest incomes, squeezed by regulatory requirements, high rents and ferocious competition from institutional and individual investors. The other group who will suffer are Irish taxpayers, who will increasingly be called upon to pay for or subvent the housing needs of a growing cohort of people, many of them migrants and refugees, who will never be able to provide accommodation for themselves from their own resources.

Migration is the Key Element in the Housing Crisis

Having provided much of the demand that created the Celtic Tiger property bubble, migration is now a major element in the demand overload that has led to the current housing crisis. How could it be otherwise? It may be abhorrent to the politically correct mind-set that high levels of migration are a major element in the housing crisis. It may be an inconvenient truth that if you add 29,200 people – the yearly net immigration figure for non-nationals in the last four years – to the indigenous population who need to be housed every year, you increase the problem significantly, but nonetheless it's true. The problem is then compounded year on year. To pretend that migration is not part of the problem is absurd. Yet every conceivable reason under the sun is advanced as being responsible for this problem, except the most obvious one – the elephant in the room – the continuing huge influx of immigrants.

What is the solution to the housing crisis? There is the obvious one of building more houses of course. If the Department of Finance figures for house completions in 2006 are to be believed – a whopping 93,400 were built – then we have done this before. The difference then was that the building was privately funded for the most part.

There is a figure which is often used of about 100,000 extra, social and affordable houses that need to be built over the next five to ten years. A substantial number of these will be required to house immigrants. At today's prices this would cost about €35 billion or say €5 billion a year, most of which would have to be bourn by the taxpayer. According to the OGCI Government of Ireland web-site, the Irish taxpayer funded public housing to the tune of €2.3 billion in 2019. Loading these huge additional costs onto the taxpayer may prove to be unacceptable when the full implications for people's pay-packets become apparent.

The alternative solution to the housing crisis, or at least part of the solution – which nobody dare mention – is to control and restrict inward migration to a reasonable figure. This would reduce demand in the property market, lowering house prices and rents. We can't expect Apple, Google, Facebook, Twitter or the other multinationals, to pay the infrastructural and social costs of importing thousands of workers – and pay their wages as well – so why not employ locals.

Every year the equivalent of the population of a large provincial town – the size of Kilkenny city – arrives in Ireland to live and work here on a permanent basis. They probably have not bought houses in advance of their arrival and they seem not to have joined the homeless on our streets. Somehow or other they have managed to secure shelter, most probably in the rented sector and quite possibly with the assistance of the taxpayer in the form of social welfare, Rental Supplement or other state assistance. They and the normal cohort of indigenous entrants to the housing market must end up being shoehorned into an inadequate supply of housing, pushing up prices and rents in the process and enduring a lot of stress and human misery. We have failed to acknowledge a key element in the housing crisis because we are in denial about the role of immigration in our society and its many implications.

The time has come to put aside ideology and wishful thinking and recognise the mathematical reality of our housing crisis. The natural increase in population here of 30,000 per year is being more than doubled by a flood of immigration – 35,800 (net) this year alone – ensuring the gap between the housing supply and the numbers to be housed is widening not narrowing. As long as this level of immigration continues – and many are working to ensure it does – housing becomes scarcer and more expensive, rents will rise and homelessness will grow. The taxpaying public will be burdened with the cost of providing subsidised accommodation for a growing proportion of the population, indigenous and immigrant alike.

8

The Debate

With the exception of Switzerland, Sweden and Austria, no country in Europe − not even Germany with its Syrian influx of 2015 − has experienced the levels of immigration per capita that have occurred in Ireland, in recent times. Nor has any country in Europe had as little meaningful discussion about this important subject. Of course there are any number of stories in the media about individual migrants and their trials and tribulations, their successes and disappointments, but that is not the same thing as a meaningful discourse on all the many aspects of migration, that impact on society in general.

Hard cases are not hard to find when it comes to individual migrants and they make great copy. Emotion and empathy can easily be stirred up and then used to silence or exclude discussion on the wider aspects of migration. The negative aspects of large-scale immigration on society are rarely if ever mentioned in this country. Someone might be offended.

We live in a world of instant emotional gratification. Public sympathy and outrage are easily manipulated when a human face is put on a tragic situation. The advertising gurus use this to great effect when they work for aid agencies and charities. Public discourse on many issues is now orchestrated in the media, in Ireland and elsewhere, on the basis of the infamous but insightful remark of Joseph Stalin that, *'one man's death is a tragedy, the death of millions is a statistic'*. A classic recent illustration of this dynamic at work was the global outrage at the murder of Jamal Khashoggi, while at the same time the world looked on with indifference at the thousands of deaths and starvation occurring in Yemen.

This personalisation strategy was very effectively deployed in our most recent referendum on abortion, where it cut the ground from under any rational argument by the opposition. The extensive use of the Halapanavar case and a few others, was more than likely decisive, in the battle for the votes of the Irish electorate. The rights of thousands of faceless, unknown, unborn children were extinguished by the skilful use of a handful of hard cases. Ireland is not alone in having abandoned the old and wise adage that 'hard cases make bad law'.

But having adopted the approach that the best way to conduct our business and formulate our laws, is to examine the hard cases, in all their exceptional, unique and bizarre detail, and on that basis, to make our decisions about what's best for everyone – we can now proceed with confidence and apply these principles to the migration issue. The personal tragedies of a few well publicised cases can now fundamentally influence or change public policy and have done so. For example, the Aylan Kurdi case, the three-year-old washed up on a Mediterranean beach, in a failed migration bid, caused outrage in Europe and was a significant element in the renewal of public support for Merkel's Syrian invitation when it faltered in September 2015. This strategy has been used to great effect by the pro-migration lobby to justify an open door policy, with little regard for any negative or unintended societal consequences.

The Trojan Horse

The first port of call for the committed activist in any public discussion, is now the personalisation of the issue. This is the Trojan Horse that can overthrow logic, reason and common sense. Consideration of facts, the implications for the common good and the future consequences of precedents set on foot of very particular circumstances, are all overwhelmed by the tragic and the poignant. There is no longer room for the objective, careful consideration of the factors in a situation. This is the precarious analytical process we have allowed to be foisted upon ourselves, under the direction of the esteemed maestros of manipulation.

The forensic examination and analysis of the general principles, effects and implications of large-scale immigration on our society has fallen victim to this new approach. Apart from the odd letter to the newspapers and a few journalists who have written courageously about the subject, little or no objective discussion, critical analysis or public discourse has taken place on this issue or the underlying principles or effects involved. On a matter of immense public importance there has been a deafening silence.

Serious consideration of the issue is mostly confined to the very occasional academic 'study' which makes its way into the papers. An article in the *Sunday Times* on 24th September 2017[(1)] entitled *'Women and young people are more negative on immigration'*, quoted one such study by the ESRI and Trinity College Dublin on the question of immigration and Ireland's boom and bust. From the article, the study appears, in the first instance to be an examination of why different groups of people have more negative attitudes to immigration than others. The first question that comes to mind, on reading the heading is, are people always required to have positive attitudes to immigration? After identifying the problems of the different groups – unemployment and financial difficulties mainly – the study found that these groups linked their problems to immigration. This should be no surprise to anyone familiar with the workings of the labour market, where women and young people are often in competition with migrants in the areas of retail, hotel and restaurant, administrative and service sectors, which are often low paid.

This study also draws at least two other obvious conclusions. The first was that *'there was no anti-immigration right-wing party in the period (2002-2012) in Ireland'* which is undoubtedly true. The coupling of 'anti-immigration' and 'right-wing' here is significant and indicative of an ingrained bias against those whose views do not accord with the liberal consensus. What has become of the objectivity we are entitled to expect from our academic institutions like Trinity and the ESRI? *'Anti-immigration'* and *'right wing'* like the old song says of *'love'* and *'marriage'* seem to be an inseparable pair, like that other famous duo *'liberal'* and *'democracy'*. The use of *'anti-immigration right-wing'* or *'far-right'* labels, has become the dismissive description of anyone who expresses any doubts about the merits of immigration.

On the question of there being no political party raising the issue of large-scale immigration, it would be a serious misjudgement, to think that many, if not most people in this country are not concerned about it. On the apparent lack of dissenters to the liberal stance on migration – there is no lack of dissenters – it is just that they cannot be heard, they've been censored, redacted. In an age of diversity, the only political game in town that is tolerated is the liberal 'progressive' agenda. Diversity does not seem to apply to political views.

The study's other reported conclusion was that *'anti-immigrant discourse is not present in the media'*, which is also evident to anyone who read a newspaper or listened to a broadcast here in the last twenty years. Most people do not want to see or indulge in, anti-immigrant discourse. However, anti-immigrant discourse is not the same thing as opposition to large-scale immigration.

What many people do want is discussion, debate and critical analysis of all aspects, negative as well as positive, of the fundamentally important issue of large-scale inward migration. The conditions for such a debate have been compromised by the hysterical rantings of uber-liberal groups who seek to shout down and intimidate anyone who raises this issue. Cyber-bullying, intimidation, personal abuse and threats are the price of raising this issue and the risk of incurring this kind of treatment, has successfully stifled debate. Consequently, the public discourse on the subject has been reduced to recounting the personal experiences of a handful of individuals, the good outcomes for some and the hostility encountered by others. This is no substitute for a real, substantive debate on migration.

Anti-immigrant versus anti-migration

The most important thing the study referred to earlier tells us, is indicated by the language its authors choose to use, which is typical of much of the discussion on the subject. The use of the term 'anti-immigrant' is an absolutely crucial point in understanding the nature of the debate on migration in Ireland. When the study says that *'anti-immigrant discourse is not present in the media'* it is immediately personalising, subjectifying the argument and applying it to the individual migrant. It is also missing the point about the most important aspect of the migration issue.

Anti-immigrant sentiment is a personal antipathy towards immigrants. Anti-immigrant sentiment regretfully does exist. But the argument we need to have is not about whether we like individual immigrants or not. The argument we need to have is whether we are prepared to allow large-scale immigration or not.

The important question here is the distinction between 'anti-immigrant' and 'anti-migration'. They are not the same thing.

Anti-immigrant sentiment is personal. Anti-migration sentiment is about social, economic and cultural policy. It is the belief that migration numbers for a particular community or country have been exceeded and further migration should be tightly controlled. It has nothing to do with whether one likes immigrants or not. This is a fundamentally important distinction. The deliberate attempt to conflate these two very different standpoints is widespread in the media here and, intentionally or not, it appears to be the case in this study from academia too. It is the basis on which public discourse on migration is being incorrectly linked – and deliberately so – to xenophobia and racism. This is the excuse the media and others use to impose their blanket censorship on public discussion of this topic. It is the clarion call to liberal extremism, to the righteously outraged, to the heretic burning mob – the call to silence dissent.

The subjectification of the argument about immigration by the use of the term 'anti-immigrant discourse' means that objective logic cannot be brought to bear on the subject. It seeks to place discussion of this issue firmly on a basis of personal antipathy towards migrants. Western legal systems have always endeavoured to view things objectively. That is why disputes and trials are conducted by judges and juries who are scrupulously chosen so that they have no connection to victims, plaintiffs or defendants. They must be totally objective if they are to reach fair and just decisions. Imagine the sort of justice that would be dispensed if the victims of crime, coming from a subjective point of view, tried cases and imposed punishments.

The personalisation of the migration debate has been successful so far in Ireland. A large part of the media and the considerable NGO and human rights industry, would like this to continue and work hard on the emotions of the population to ensure that it does. The Irish inclination, an almost genetic predisposition to side with the underdog, leaves many people vulnerable to manipulation by the appeal of solidarity with the downtrodden. As in any human situation, there is never any shortage of tragedy, misfortune and heartbreak in the stories of refugees and migrants. The difficulty with having a rational debate on migration is that emotion will always trump reason, especially in the hands of skilful manipulators with an agenda.

The often used phrase 'the struggle for the hearts and minds of the people', rightly puts hearts before minds. No television or radio show worth its salt today is without the shedding of a few tears or the breaking voice. A classic example of the power of emotion, with massive repercussions occurred in July 2015 when German Chancellor Merkel encountered a young Palestinian girl on a live television show in Rostock, who was anxious that her family might be deported from Germany. When Merkel did not give her the assurance that the family would not be deported she began to cry. It was the kind of moment packed with drama and pathos, that television producers would kill for, and it was a huge embarrassment for Merkel. She was widely criticised in Germany for her failure to respond 'appropriately'. By the end of the following month she had redeemed herself by issuing that infamous invitation to Syrian refugees which soon had a million respondents. The Rostock encounter may not have been the lynchpin for the invasion, but it primed the detonator.

If the Germans are vulnerable to emotional weakness then the Irish are doubly so. When the Germans recovered their composure and began to appreciate the full implications of their emotional breakdown, they quickly moved to share out the burden of their impulsive generosity and wasted no time in plugging the leak in the Greek border with Turkish help. Within weeks of the invitation being issued, the heart was being challenged by the mind and – luckily for all of us in Europe – the mind was reasserting its primacy. Vociferous criticism of the new migration policy and the disorder that followed engendered swift and decisive action. The

Schengen shambles was halted and under the pressure of sharing the influx, members got their act together and order was restored to some degree. Given our own feeble record in migration management and our vulnerability to emotional blackmail, I shudder to think what might have happened if we had been put in the same position as the Germans.

The Underdog Factor

Twenty five years ago, when the Irish mass migration saga started, the political, business and media establishment were all in favour and that remains the case to this day. There was never any serious or sustained criticism of migration policy here or indeed, any in-depth analysis of the effects of large-scale immigration on the economy or society. The media-enforced gagging order has held firm throughout the period, unlike in Britain or on the Continent. Despite the depth of the crisis here in 2008, that consensus was never broken and the connection between economic meltdown and migration was never made. The taboo remains firmly in place.

The Irish inclination to side with the underdog is only part of the emotional bondage that allows the mass migration taboo to escape critical analysis. The other great trauma in the national psyche, referred to previously, is the Irish encounter with emigration. The idea that in the relatively recent past, we often reared our children for export is still a painful reality for most Irish people. The stories of lonely, desperate and exploited lives spent scrubbing floors or digging trenches in some foreign land are part of the family history for many. This makes the Irish slow to criticise or question migration. In the spirit of 'do unto others as you would have them do unto you', we are loath to offend the stranger or refuse him or her access.

While this is generous and laudable up to a point, we have gone way beyond that point at this stage. What has happened here is that our good nature has been taken advantage of and our generosity has been abused. We have allowed a self-serving clique at the top of our society, who have profited greatly from the influx, aided and abetted by a liberal elite in thrall to political correctness, to hijack the economy and society, in their own interests. An integral part of this new reality is large-scale immigration, which is part of the machinery of cost control, competitiveness, increased productivity and consumption on the economic front and societal, demographic and cultural transformation.

The considerable emotional and historical baggage of the Irish has combined with other cultural influences prevalent in Europe today, such as guilt for colonial exploitation and economic success and a loss of cultural confidence. These and other factors impede our ability to see clearly where we are going. The European inferiority complex has embraced multiculturalism because it has lost faith in its own culture. It has lost believe in itself and its values. In this cloud of confusion and self-doubt, political correctness reigns supreme.

Due in no small part to our emotional predisposition on the downtrodden and the restrictions placed on free speech by the diktats of political correctness, the dice is loaded heavily against rational debate on the migration issue in Ireland. In fact, as things stand, debate on this issue of any kind, rational or otherwise seems impossible. This was also the case in Europe up to a few years ago.

The Populist Revolt

As the flow of economic migrants and asylum seekers into Europe increased, so did concern about the levels of migration. This manifested itself in the early 2000s by the emergence of political parties in places like Holland, who were opposed to uncontrolled migration. They had widespread support and would probably have formed a government in Holland in 2002, had their leader Pym

Fortuyn not been assassinated a week before the election. They represented a section of liberal opinion that had become concerned by the hostility of certain Islamic and traditional groups of migrants to Dutch views and values relating to gay rights, women's rights and other issues. Curiously, this schism in liberal thinking helped to bring about the birth of modern populism. Concern for liberal values, usually associated with the left, fused with, what one might call working-class concern about economic displacement, national identity and cultural erosion. Soon support for similar parties emerged in Denmark, Sweden, Germany, Italy, Austria and the National Front in France. Despite the opposition of the establishment, the debate about mass migration in Europe had begun in earnest.

While the Dutch liberal splinter group joined the populists, the main liberal block continued to be pro-migration, globalist, free-market and politically correct.

A decade later, as the migration crisis worsened in the Mediterranean in 2014-15 the media were all over it. The desperation, distress and human misery made great copy and dramatic footage. The unrelenting pressure eventually brought about the Merkel invitation and the mother of all unintended consequences, in that more than half the arrivals were economic migrants and not Syrian refugees. When the 2015 mass migration episode occurred, it dominated the news for months on end. A by-product of this momentous event was the heightened awareness of large-scale immigration all over Europe and the growth of the anti-immigration political parties.

The media maintained the pro-immigration, liberal orthodoxy and continued to relentlessly attack and campaign against what they contemptuously called 'far-Right' and 'Populist' political parties. In this they were articulating the views of the political, business and liberal establishments. Their efforts to crush populism or at least bring it to a temporary halt, might well have been successful but for the 2015 mass migration episode.

Two devastating hammer blows followed for the liberal elite consensus soon after 2015, in the form of the Brexit and Trump victories. Despite this they have regrouped and continue their efforts to subvert those decisions of the electorate, with some success.

The Media Takes Sides

The issue which dominated these two political campaigns (Brexit and Trump) was migration. The print and particularly the broadcast media in Britain were largely against Brexit, with a few exceptions, as were the vast majority of journalists. Trump was overwhelmingly opposed by journalists in the print media and by broadcasters with one or two exceptions. However, despite the deep misgivings of the journalistic profession, a debate of sorts took place and to the consternation of the establishment and the 'progressive' elites, the people had their say.

The Irish media on the other hand were not going to lend a hostage to fortune in the form of diversity of views. Right from the start, having nailed their colours to the pro-migration mast, they failed in their role as facilitator for robust and unbiased debate. They acted as censor and protagonist in a contest where they should have been scrupulously neutral. Using the traditional weapons of shame and guilt which had been so effective in the past, with generous dollops of moral outrage, they succeeded in imposing a gagging order on the subject of migration.

Despite the many negative aspects of the mass migration experience in Ireland, negative comment or critical analysis of the subject is not facilitated. Even the term 'mass migration' is forbidden as a description of what has happened here. The 'group think' that has enveloped the media on this particular topic is a spectacular illustration of *'a strong group that continues to set the boundaries of permissible views'*, to quote Breda O'Brien from *The Irish Times* again[2].

The subject of large-scale immigration is highly controversial. It is now so fraught with guilt that people who approach it feel impelled to apologise in advance for expressing an opinion, which might not accord fully with the conventional view. An example of this appeared in David Quinn's article in the *Sunday Times* 1st October 2017 [3], where he refreshingly gets to grips with the real issues in relation to migration. However, before he starts, he tells us, *'for the record'*, that he's married to a non-EU migrant, which presumably gives him a kind of special permission to speak on the subject.

The prohibition on discussing migration and the requirement for special leave to discuss it is not just an Irish phenomenon. A senior international expert on migration, Paul Collier in the opening remarks of his book *Exodus* also informs us of the multinational nature of his family, presumably as an assertion of his fitness to speak on the subject. While this is understandable, it indicates a lamentable constraint on free speech, where those who propose to speak, must parade their special qualifications before expressing themselves.

The implication for the rest of us, with no special dispensation, is presumably that we have little or no right to have an opinion on this fundamental issue. The philosophy of political correctness, that dominates opinion in the Western media today, is strongly of the view – that immigration is a matter in which the public have no say whatsoever.

With this in mind and having pulled down the shutters on free speech, in the interest of the public good, no doubt, the media in Ireland have decided not to facilitate any public debate on this issue. In fact they have decided to go even further and lead the charge against those who do raise it. The progressive tendency in the press and broadcast media have been quick to interpret concern about mass migration as attempting to stir up the 'politics of fear' and those who raise it are invariably dismissed as 'far right'.

The Left joins the Mob

When passion and conviction get out of hand, as it has with Political Correctness, the result is extremism. When extremism takes over, there is no respect or tolerance for other people's views or opinions. This appears to be what is happening on the Liberal Left in Ireland. A clique of self-righteous zealots appear to have made themselves available, in the role of 'progressive' brown-shirts, to enforce the diktats of political correctness in regard to migration. They have decreed that any discussion on migration control *'can't happen here'* because they will not allow it. They have decided that any such discussion is automatically racist and xenophobic and is therefore 'verboten'. They have, of course, no objection to free speech − for which we are very grateful − but it has to be the right kind of free speech[4].

This 'qualified' free speech, Irish style, is the sort of free speech that some on the left of the Irish political spectrum and most of the political and media establishment believes in. It's the sort of free speech that excludes views and opinions with which they disagree. In this case, views that are shared by about of half the electorate in the United States and Britain and doubtless a great number of Europeans including many Irish, on the subject of large-scale immigration.

The militant faction of the liberal 'left' take a very dim view of anyone with the temerity to raise the migration issue when they know full well that such things should not be spoken of here. The implied threat is usually enough to halt any discussion on banned topics. If however it fails, a campaign of cyber thuggery can be employed which is usually very effective. This is the kind of thing that has now become commonplace and is usually successful in halting debate. Nor is it just an Irish phenomenon. There have been numerous examples in universities in Europe and the United States where 'anti-fascist' groups, using classic fascist tactics, set out to intimidate, harass and silence those with whom they disagree – in the name of freedom!

The disturbing thing about this attempt to enforce a form of 'qualified' free speech, is that it is not an aspiration confined to the 'militant left'. In Ireland we are ahead of the curve in this regard. The recent Irish referenda have exposed a concerted effort on the part of an alliance of activist groups, highly motivated individuals and the mainstream media to drown out any dissent from the liberal consensus view of the world. Unlike the black shirts, the brown shirts and blue shirts of old, their weapon of choice is social media and cyber bullying.

These tactics have been frighteningly effective in Ireland where they have been used extensively to push the 'quiet revolution' of socially 'progressive' reforms. The result is that a rigid political consistency has been imposed with regard to the liberal consensus across all the political parties in the state. Politicians are running scared of taking a stand on anything that might be interpreted as contravening that consensus. The aftermath of the gay marriage and the abortion referenda illustrated the point, when the full spectrum of politicians turned up when the results were declared, to be seen to approve of such great leaps forward. The euphoria in the media was unbounded, as was the barely concealed contempt for the 35 per cent of 'deplorables' who voted against these propositions.

Sermons from the Moral High Ground

Unlike the recent socially 'progressive' reforms, the liberal consensus project on migration has a long history. It became an article of faith at the time of the birth of the Celtic Tiger. It came of age with the accession of the ten new members of the EU in 2004, when the steady stream of arrivals became a flood. Its finest hour was in that golden age of excess just before the crash in 2008. Despite the crash the influx continued and today the flow is steady and strong. Its supporters and defenders populate the senior ranks of the Irish media and the business, government and academic establishment.

Any threat to this consensus is likely be swiftly and effectively dealt with. So enthusiastic were the media about immigration that they entered into a bidding war of outrage when it became a political issue briefly in January 2006. With the Irish mass migration epic at its peak – there were 1,500 a week arriving – Joseph O'Malley in the Sunday Independent on 22nd Jan 2006 [(5)] took serious issue with Pat Rabbitte TD, then leader of the Labour Party and Ned O'Keeffe TD, for drawing attention to a 'problem' with our immigration policy.

This was no 'belt of a crosier' wielded by some irate bishop in the vain hope of calling a wayward flock to order. This was an exocet missile and it hit the mark. The legitimate concerns that had been articulated by Rabbitte and O'Keefe sank without trace, never to be seen again. So effective was the strike that no politician and very few others, have ever entered that territory since. While the great migration debate rages everywhere else, there is not so much as a whimper in Ireland about it.

There appeared to be almost total unanimity about the requirement for hundreds of thousands of migrants to service the Celtic Tiger economy. Brendan Keenan's article in the *Irish Independent* on 8 July 2004 was entitled 'Wanted: army of migrants to keep the Tiger purring'. Two years later it was 'Boom will be fuelled by a million immigrants', again Brendan Keenan writing in the *Irish Independent* on 23 March 2006. Bill Tyson's article in the *Irish Independent* on 25 January 2006 was 'Influx of workers gives big boost to property'. Brian Dowling's piece in the *Irish Independent* 24 January 2006 was entitled 'What we need by 2016...300,000 more'. Paul Melia in the Irish Independent 22nd October 2007, within sight of the crash, enthused 'Rainbow nation: immigrant numbers double to 420,000 as Ireland becomes multi-cultural'. And there were many more. These were fairly typical of the media consensus at the apex of the mass migration epic. No consideration was given to any possible negative impacts and dare anyone say there might be any. Despite the flood of migration into Ireland from 2005 to 2008 being considerably in excess of the German influx of 2015, the enthusiasm of the media never faltered.

The capitulation of the vast majority of Irish politicians to the agenda of 'progressive' liberalism, when they should have challenged the wisdom of allowing the aforementioned army of migrants into the country, has deepened public cynicism towards politics and politicians. This has been accompanied by a serious loss of trust in the media. When humility might have been more appropriate to our commentators, in the wake of the role they played in cheerleading the madness of the Celtic Tiger period, they continued to exert enormous influence over the political, social and economic agenda in Ireland, in the period after the crash and to this day. Part of that influence is an insistence that any suggestion that migration should be controlled is racist. To be deemed racist is the equivalent of being excommunicated in the past. It's a powerful weapon which can be fatal to a political career. Most politicians would rather encounter the black-death than an accusation of racism, which is why immigration is the elephant in the room, the unmentionable. While there is little sign at the moment that this taboo will be shattered, only time will tell. The Irish public may already be in the process of losing patience with the media and their taboos, as has already happened in many Western countries.

The Global Individualist

Part of the liberal view of the world appears to be the belief that everyone has the right to locate themselves anywhere they like. It is a principle that has found its way into mainstream politics in the form of the EU's four freedoms of movement − of people, capital, goods and services. It places the EU, its structures, laws and institutions at the service of globalism and the free market. While the free movement of capital, goods and services can facilitate trade, the free movement of people globalises and liberalises the labour market. In developed countries, it undermines the power of workers to win better wages and conditions. The free flow of labour floods the market with migrants and initiates a race to the bottom for wages and conditions. This is the implacable law of the market. The dynamics of the labour market were plainly seen in the Celtic Tiger phenomenon and the crash which followed. Despite the recovery, real wages and living standards have been more or less stagnant for the past eleven years. With the strongly growing influx of migrants, labour market conditions will more than likely continue to be depressed into the future. In contrast, in Britain, despite the threat of Brexit, the implacable law of the market continues to assert itself. With fewer migrants arriving and others returning home, wages are rising and unemployment is falling because the labour market is tightening.

Here in Ireland the notion of free movement of people is not just confined to the EU. Ireland is a true globalist when it comes to inward migration. Of the net 33,900 non-nationals who came to live and work here in 2018, a net 20,900 were from outside the EU. We are effectively operating an open door to the world when it comes to migration.

Despite the enormous ramifications of mass migration, no electorate in the developed world has ever been asked its opinion on the subject until recently. David Cameron was continuously castigated in the media for reluctantly holding a referendum on

British membership of the EU, as if some things are too important to be put to the people. Elitists are always horrified by the loss of control involved in the democratic process. The idea of letting the people decide the great issues is alien to them. They are happier lobbying and manipulating their minions in the parliaments of the world. This could be clearly seen in the three year shambles that was played out in the British Parliament in relation to Brexit. Migration was the key issue in the Brexit and Trump victories and this was the only time the public had a say on the matter. These victories were remarkable, in that they were achieved against all the odds and all the pressure and influence neo-liberalism, the political establishment and the media could muster against them. The elites fully expected to win and the shock of defeat was profound.

Conformity the Easy Option

While, for the moment in Ireland, the prospect of a political shock of these proportions seems very remote, it is inconceivable that this can remain the case forever. In the United States and Britain the liberal consensus and political correctness have been overturned and the 'deplorables' have had their say. A major concern of voters in these countries and in the West generally is large-scale immigration.

Just before the crash, in an opinion poll published in *The Irish Times* on 10 September 2008 (and referred to earlier)[6], 66 per cent of the Irish people said they wanted a tighter immigration policy. Eleven years and an economic catastrophe later we are still waiting. At least part of the reason for our failure to act on immigration is that we are acutely vulnerable to the notion of guilt. In common with globalists elsewhere, the liberal consensus here has come to the view that migration is good. A continuous, unrelenting campaign supports this idea, to the point where it is unthinkable to believe otherwise. With the Irish weakness for the comfort of conformity and a partisan press implacably opposed to discussing the subject, Ireland stands alone as the only society in the developed world to fail to acknowledge that migration might pose a problem. The Irish people want a tighter immigration policy, but – like Hamlet – not enough to put aside their scruples, get over their misplaced guilt and the media monkey on their back and do something about it.

We have been made to believe that opposition to immigration is not only bad, it is racist, fascist and xenophobic. This makes opposition to immigration not only bad, but evil. This is the view of our betters, the enlightened view. Our strong conformist streak, evident in the gay marriage referendum campaign, where dissenters were very hard to find, bids us in public at least, to dutifully nod assent, whatever we may think in private. Anything for a quiet life and who wants to carry the guilt of denying the migrating masses the chance of a better life, no matter what the consequences for ourselves? Who in Ireland wants to be a 'deplorable' redneck or a far-right populist?

The conformist atmosphere of the past in Ireland is now viewed with horror and dismay by the enlightened commentators of today. The perception of the priest-ridden society of sixty years ago is the subject of much scorn and derision. In fact it would be hard to find anyone to defend it, even in the Church. In a curious way, this generally accepted view of that time – the conformity to the Catholic ethos that brooked no dissent – is mirrored in the intellectual intolerance of today. The new secular ascendency is equally dismissive of dissent and with its television assistant in the corner of every living-room, it is far more effective in enforcing conformity. The priest-ridden populace of the past is replaced by a neoliberalism-ridden populace of the present, with an agenda that is equally, if not more intolerant. Thus the conformity of the past survives, coming full circle.

In this atmosphere it is hardly surprising that debate on such an heretical issue as large-scale immigration is virtually absent. The equivalent, sixty years ago, would be a debate on gay marriage or abortion. The few token dissenters that are tolerated today, have received a special dispensation on foot of special personal circumstances but the ban remains resolutely in place for the rest of us. The new 'progressive elite', in the same paternalistic spirit of the past, have taken it upon themselves to ensure that we do not stray from the path of righteousness.

While debate in Ireland on migration is almost non-existent, it has become the number one issue in the Western world. It features prominently on television news services on an almost nightly basis. It's at, or near the top of the political agenda in parliaments all over Europe and the West. There are populist senior ministers and even prime-ministers in some EU countries. The attempt by the media, politicians and the liberal establishment to exclude those who oppose mass migration as 'far-right' or 'populist' still continues but has failed utterly. Recent elections have given a clear indication that voters want this problem addressed urgently and are prepared to vote for those who will address it. European governments who were reluctant to tackle this problem have been forced by voters to regard migration control as a top priority.

Large-scale immigration is an existential issue for the EU and with more than 55million migrants (UN Migration Report 2017), not including their children born on the continent, who could amount to another 50 million, mass migration is the appropriate description of what has been happening. Unless it is resolved satisfactorily with effective controls, it could destroy the whole European Union project. This was clearly visible during the migrant crisis of 2015, when some EU members from Eastern Europe refused point blank to accept, what they believed were economic migrants masquerading as refugees, as they still do today. A rift has opened up between Eastern and Western Europe on the issue. As the crisis of 2015 developed, the Schengen agreement fell into disarray. The ever increasing power of the EU has been rejected by the United Kingdom because its citizens believe it has undermined their democracy and their ability to make their own decisions. Whether the UK leaves or not, huge damage has been done to the EU and the fragile support for it has been further eroded. As a relatively low level migrant crisis continues and global instability increases, a new mass migration episode could erupt at any time, shattering the Schengen agreement and weakening the EU still further.

The debate about migration now raging in Europe and America looks for the moment to have been successfully stifled in Ireland. We remain firmly anchored in the mire of denial. A rock solid pro-migration consensus seems set to continue for the foreseeable future and with our record on conformity this may well be the case. By the time we wake up to the transformation that has overwhelmed us, it may be too late to do anything about it. We may well find ourselves in that old familiar role of dancing to someone else's tune and perhaps, deep down, maybe that's what we want. After seven hundred years of colonial oppression and barely fifty years of independence, we enthusiastically handed back much of our sovereignty to the EU. Perhaps James Joyce was right when he described us as *'the gratefully oppressed'*.

9

Social Cohesion

For the cosmopolitan liberal in Ireland today – and who would admit to being anything else – ethnicity is an archaic irrelevance. The liberal disposition has no need of tribal labels, they are citizens of the world. They are supporters of the progressive agenda and their views and opinions dominate the public discourse, here and in the West generally. They have our politician's attention and their issues are the ones that will be addressed. The progressive tendency is very keen on equality, as long as it is not the kind of equality that threatens their pre-eminent position and their dominance of politics and society. As we have seen over the last three years, there is an important distinction between equality with poorly educated insular Brexiteers and Trump supporters on the one hand, and progressive equality on the other. To the progressive liberal, immigration is a desirable development, providing a hardworking, cheaper, pliant and more reliable alternative to the lower orders of natives.

In general migrants do not challenge or compete with the top strata of society. Few migrants grace the boardrooms of top Irish companies, despite the enthusiasm of business for migration. Nor do they figure prominently in the top echelons of the civil service or in the professions, apart perhaps, in medicine and academia. Even if many are well educated, the networks at the top of our society are difficult to penetrate. When the vast majority of migrants arrive, they invariably settle in poorer communities where rents are cheaper and the cost of living is lower, so their presence has little or no impact on the better off. When they compete for jobs, it is with the lower orders at the bottom end of the job market. When their children go to school, their lack of English language proficiency does not impede the progress of the children of the elite. Usually they do not attend fee paying schools. There are no personal negative aspects to migration for the top strata.

The drift towards multiculturalism and globalisation is not seen as a threat to the well off. They have the marketable skills, educational attainments and connections to make their way anywhere. They embrace these developments as an opportunity to further their own individual agenda. Nations and societies are but a context in which their own personal drama is played out. For the top strata, race and tribe means little or nothing.

In sharp contrast, in migrant communities, race, tribe and family are of the utmost importance. The impulse to congregate in particular locations is a consequence of this and is a longstanding tendency that is unlikely to change, clearly evident in every host country on the planet. It is perfectly logical that people of similar origin and background should form their own communities, establish their own networks and pool their own resources – perfectly logical, except perhaps to the liberal individualist. To the migrant, in a sometimes hostile environment, the security and protection of the community and the tribe is almost always welcome.

The impact of the tendency to congregate in particular locations by migrants has important implications for migrants themselves and the host communities. In Britain, for the poorer natives who are the original inhabitants of these areas, the migrant impulse to congregate may lead to them becoming a minority in their own locality. They can become cultural and ethnic outsiders on their own turf. As pressure increases on accommodation with more new arrivals, space and resources decline and costs and rents rise. Many of the original natives, particularly the young, if they can, will leave the area. This is the beginning of ghettoisation, a process that seems to go hand in hand with large-scale immigration.

The Migrant Accommodation Mystery

When the Irish emigrated to the United States and Britain in the past, they congregated in enclaves in the large cities as migrants from the developing countries do in Europe today. The extent to which this happens in Ireland is as yet unclear. Where or how, the large numbers of migrants that arrive here every year, are accommodated or housed is a mystery which might well benefit from some scrutiny, in light of the current housing crisis.

It is widely suspected that vast amounts of public money is spent by government agencies, taxpayer funded charities, NGOs and others, on the provision of accommodation to non-nationals arriving into this country. A recent example of how this works was referred to in a local paper in 2018. According to a report in the *Meath Chronicle* on the 10th July 2018[1], a Cluid development of sixty-seven houses opened in Ashbourne, County Meath, for people on the housing list, the previous week. The average waiting time for the new occupiers was seven years, with one individual waiting twenty years. Seven of the houses were allocated to Syrian families who probably were relatively new arrivals, which were presumably funded by the taxpayer.

There is no evidence that the substantial financial resources required to house many of those that arrive here, are brought with them. If this is indeed the case, then the people who are paying for it, the taxpayers, are entitled to know, in the spirit of transparency, what exactly is happening. The Housing Assistance Payments (HAP) bill for county Meath alone (in 2017) was €7.5 million[2], indicating that the national bill is likely to be in the region of €180 million, one third of which assists non-nationals with their rents. There are currently around 72,000 households on the waiting list, to be housed presumably with taxpayer assistance. One quarter of these are non-national households. These are some of the questions that we must ponder if we are to make informed decisions about the benefits or otherwise of large-scale inward migration.

If it is not the case that many migrants depend on publicly funded housing, then can we have the facts? The public should be provided with an explanation of how an enormous number of poor people can arrive in a high cost economy, with few resources or connections and provide accommodation and the means of living for themselves and their families at no cost to the taxpayer. Part of the reason why the public is not being made aware of the facts behind this extraordinary state of affairs, is perhaps that it might reflect badly on the chaotic lack of migration policy of this state and encourage discussion of the wider topic with a view to controlling and reducing the influx.

What is clear about migrant accommodation is that very few end up on the street. Where or how they find accommodation in a country in a severe housing crisis is a mystery, if not a miracle. More than 10,000 people are designated as homeless in Ireland and more than seven times that number are on local authority housing lists all over the country. There are probably tens of thousands more living with parents or relatives who need their own accommodation. Yet the equivalent of four large towns, a total 117,000 non-nationals (net) have arrived in Ireland in the last four years and been somehow accommodated, including almost 36,000 in 2019 alone. This is a conundrum that requires an explanation. Are the Irish public, many of whom are unable to afford a house themselves, supposed to pay for accommodation for a growing cohort of migrants through their taxes?

Multiculturalism and the Ghetto

The downside of the migrant impulse to congregate is the phenomenon of ghettoisation. Many ethnic groups in Britain and Europe have, over the years, gathered in enclaves in the large cities, to form separate, often mono-cultural ethnic communities. Given the level of immigration occurring into Ireland today, the cost of rents in Dublin, where many settle and the kind of incomes they have from jobs or social welfare, the process of ghettoisation may well begin to emerge in Ireland in the near future, if it has not already started. Indications from the populations of some primary schools where over two thirds of the pupils are non-nationals, suggest that the north inner city of Dublin, half a dozen west Dublin suburbs, Balbriggan, Navan, Athlone and Longford, all have high concentrations of foreign nationals.

Unlike European migration to the United States, Canada and Australia in previous centuries where migrants shared language, religious, cultural and family ties with the host countries, many of today's migrants do not have any connections with their host countries, apart possibly with migrants who have already moved there. Another crucially important difference is of course, that these countries were under populated, in stark contrast to Europe and Ireland today.

Part of the territory that goes with the ethnic enclave or the ghetto is multiculturalism. The idea of multiculturalism is often confusing and misunderstood. It is sometimes taken to mean, people of different origins and backgrounds living together in blissful harmony, a kind of benign melting pot. Unfortunately, this is usually too good to be true. When people of the same origin and background congregate in a district in a large town or city, far from home, they tend to try to recreate the culture, language (sometimes) and customs of their homeland. The location, instead of becoming multicultural, tends to become a mono-cultural ethnic enclave which can amount to a kind of self-imposed apartheid. In the United Kingdom, Europe and possibly here, some migrant communities live separate, parallel lives under traditions, customs and laws that can be at variance and sometimes in opposition to those of the country they are living in. At the extreme end, this may manifest itself as FGM (female genital mutilation), honour killings and forced marriages, but more importantly, any number of lesser, but questionable practices and attitudes, which do not accord with law and practice in the host country. A recent example, was an Irish Supreme Court ruling on a polygamous Islamic marriage due last year (2018), which would allow a Lebanese man to have two wives, thereby changing the institution of marriage to suit the requirements of Islam, which is at variance with Irish law and practice and setting an important precedent. The judges appear to have passed the buck to the legislature on this occasion. This is the tail wagging the dog and amounts to an erosion of the values and way of life for the host nation.

The multicultural approach to immigration was accepted and even encouraged by European governments up to about ten years ago. When security concerns and terrorist activity in Europe began to emerge, thinking on the multicultural approach began to change. In response to growing public concern over increasing levels of immigration and the sometimes malign influences at work in the parallel ethnic communities in the large cities, the politicians had to change their tune. In October 2010 Angela Merkel said, in a widely reported speech, that multiculturalism had 'failed utterly'[3]. Before long, Britain's David Cameron, France's Nicolas Sarkozy, and Australia's John Howard had joined in the chorus. The problem was that it was too late. These communities had already formed and the parallel way of life had become entrenched. There was no going back.

Ethnic Fuel to the Fire

The jobs and economic opportunities that brought many of these migrants to Europe in the first place, have, in many instances disappeared. They have been left high and dry as the economic tide has receded. With little to do and few prospects for advancement, resentment inevitably builds. Many of these places now exist mainly on social welfare and are a prey to the usual vices associated with poverty. With the added edge of ethnic tension augmenting the aggravation quotient, the scene is set for fireworks.

Instances of racial rioting, arson and looting have occurred in Britain, France, the United States and Sweden recently and no-go areas for the police are common all over Europe. The media are generally reluctant to report crime carried out by ethnic minorities, as was the case in Rotherham, Cologne, Stockholm and elsewhere. Instances often only come to light through social media and the internet.

Here in Ireland we are not immune to the same malady. The problems of alienation, hostility, criminality and anti-social activity are here already in spades in our own post working-class communities. If the added incendiary element of ethnicity is added to the already volatile mix in our larger towns and cities, we can expect rising levels of gang violence, lawlessness and social malaise. We are often foolishly prone to believe that such things could not happen here. When the Celtic Tiger died, many migrants lost their jobs and like their Irish counterparts joined the social welfare queues in their adopted country and were happy to do so. Their children however, when their time comes, might not be so happy to live on the margins and will make their disenchantment very plain, as they do in the European ghettoes today. There is no such thing as Irish exceptionalism when it comes to social discord. How can we seriously expect to be any different to Britain, France, Germany, Holland, Belgium or Sweden when we draw from the same globalised well of problems?

Meanwhile, life in Ireland, as in the aforementioned countries, will go on as usual for the better off. No sleep will be lost in the leafy suburbs over the plight of the huddled masses in the run down districts of cities and towns. Unless they themselves become victims of the frisson between the warring factions on the periphery of society, nothing will be done. The new element that may spur some remedial action on the migration question is the Western European experience of terrorism. Radical Islamic agitation has brought the disaffection of some of these alienated and resentful migrant communities to a new level that cannot be ignored. What other malicious radicalisms are waiting in the wings for their turn to infect Western societies, already struggling with their own problems, whose immune systems have been compromised by a loss of confidence, moral compass and self-loathing?

For the moment however, in Ireland at least, inertia, the pro-migration lobby and political correctness still impede any attempt to talk about, let alone tackle the migration issue. A steadily increasing flow of non-national migration into the country continues. Ties of family, race and obligation provide incentive and encouragement and ease the way for those at home to take the risk involved in migration. Once a bridgehead has been established the natural tendency is for the flow to increase, as was the case with the Irish in Britain and America.

Societal Erosion

The effects of this profound demographic change are far-reaching. One of those effects is the weakening of the bonds that hold society together. The point is being rapidly reached, if it has not already been surpassed, where we can no longer identify with many of the people we encounter. The people we see in our streets, shops, schools and hospitals are strangers. The feelings of loyalty and solidarity we once felt for the communities in which we grew up, or worked, or socialised or lived, have evaporated and have been replaced by feelings of indifference and more probably by suspicion. Many of us cannot identify on any but the most distant level with the new arrivals.

The environment we inhabit has lost the qualities of a society. It no longer shares a common culture, a set of common values, an ethnicity or even the same language. The bonds of familiarity, solidarity, loyalty and sympathy have been eroded. While our public bodies boast of hosting 200 different nationalities in modern Ireland, as if it were some wonderful achievement, some at least of the native population, wonder how many more foreigners it will take to satisfy the thirst for diversity of those who set the societal agenda? There is a suspicion that it is more a question of, how many more will it take to suppress their gnawing feeling of inferiority at being Irish. Meanwhile, with the continuous stream of new arrivals, those bonds become weaker. Ireland as a place with a unique character is on a suicide mission, and it is succeeding.

We can take comfort that in our desire for self-destruction we are not alone. Western Europe appears to be on the same path as ourselves, driven by the same demons of shame, inferiority and self-loathing and under the same intellectual directorship of political correctness. However, the liberal elite who are manning the helm and steering us into these turbulent waters are presiding over an increasingly impatient and rebellious crew, in Europe at least. A populist mutiny, with all the many perils that that may entail, may be the only hope for resolving Europe's identity crisis.

Meanwhile, everything remains tranquil in the emerald isle, or so it appears. The ban – we were always good at bans – on any real debate about migration, is now in place for more than twenty years and is still managing to keep the lid on dissent. However, the promotion of migration as a self-evident and unquestionable good is wearing thin, even here. Alternative sources of information, on the internet and elsewhere, are exposing the shortcomings and inconsistencies in the liberal narrative on migration.

The Price of Mass Migration

What might eventually expose the myth of this unquestionable good may be the economic cost. Housing, infrastructure and services are three critical areas already in crisis and unable to meet current demand. If the levels of net migration – more than 30,000 a year – of the last three years are sustained, then massive amounts of Irish taxpayer's money will be required to upgrade infrastructure, provide housing and revamp services such as health and education not to mention social welfare and pensions. These levels of net inward migration for non-nationals look likely to be not only sustained but to accelerate in the coming years. Last year the net increase was from 33,900 to 35,800 individuals. These services are already struggling and require large amounts of additional resources every year just to stand still. Health expenditure in 2016 was €14.1 billion, in 2020 it will be €18.33 billion and the bill for education has risen by 20 per cent over the same period to €11.19 billion[3]. The likelihood is that the deterioration that has been evident in recent times will continue, despite continuously increasing expenditure. Waiting times in hospitals will increase, school places and public and private housing will be scarcer and social welfare and pensions will not keep pace with inflation. The overall effect, particularly on the bottom half of society, is that real living standards will decline.

Public disquiet about deteriorating services, housing shortages and overstretched resources were a key factor in the UK electorate's decision to leave the EU. Fundamental to that decision was the belief that large-scale immigration was being facilitated by EU policies and laws, with little regard for local concerns. The UK electorate is not alone in its scepticism about the EU. People all over Europe are beginning to draw the same conclusions about the massive costs involved in maintaining decent healthcare and education services, social housing and welfare, in the face of large-scale immigration.

In Ireland we are still some way from fully appreciating these costs, partly because of the failure of analysis and robust debate that should be taking place. Much is made of the contribution of migrants to the economy and it is undoubtedly true that cheap migrant labour has greatly benefited the competitiveness and profitability of many Irish businesses. This however, is not the same as benefiting society as a whole. Apart from the widespread misleading bias in the media on immigration, a serious shortfall in information, statistics and facts about the costs of immigration to the Irish economy, is hampering an informed debate. The real costs – inclusive of health, education, social welfare, pensions and housing – of hosting almost a million migrants, must be balanced against their real economic contribution to our society, before we can say whether immigration is a good thing or not, from an economic point of view.

Another factor in our failure to fully appreciate the costs of immigration is the slightly subversive attitude, part of our colonial heritage perhaps, widely held in some sections of society, that public money is free money – manna from heaven as it were. This is well illustrated by a recent government decision to fund the care of a group of forty Middle-Eastern teenagers from the Calais camp. The cost involved was €10 million for the first year or an eye-watering €250,000 for each individual[4]. This is eight times the average industrial wage or enough to put them up in the best hotel in Ireland for the year with change to spare! Presumably the money will go to fund a plethora of organisations supplying, no doubt, vital services to the teenagers – at great expense, as most publicly funded projects tend to be – and not to the individuals themselves. Before the Syrian war these young people were probably living on less than €2,500 a year, 100 times less than the Irish taxpayer will be paying for their upkeep. This grossly extravagant plan was agreed by Dail Eireann without demur and apparently accepted by the public without question. This is the kind of financial insanity that is endemic in Dail Eireann. Manna from heaven it must be.

Of course this malaise is not just confined to politicians. The penny has not yet dropped with some sections of the Irish public, that government money is their money and should not be wasted. When it does, perhaps a bit more reason and a little less emotion and outrage will inform our debates. We need to be a lot less approving of the awarding of large wads of taxpayers' money to all and sundry for 'good' causes – like the Calais teenagers – and trivial or imagined wrongs, invariably the fault of the state, in the absence of any other convenient, well-funded culprit. The fashionable obsession with victimhood and its counterpart, the allocation of blame, which is a major part of the media landscape today, does a serious disservice to real victims. Many of us still seem to feel, like obstreperous teenagers, that anyone putting one over on the state is a cause for celebration, when in fact we are shooting ourselves in the foot. Every euro the state spends comes out of our own pocket and should be well spent. We must extend this rigorous analysis to our assessment of the costs and benefits of immigration to our society as a whole. It is not just about facilitating that portion of society, who are in a position to take advantage of cheap labour and increased demand for whatever they are making or selling. We must join in the European-wide discussion on the effects of migration on our societies at every level.

The idea that this great debate about migration is essentially a manifestation of latent racism, is an attempt to impose a politically correct stranglehold on free speech. It attempts to constrain a vital debate about the nature and dynamics of society and the fractures and fault-lines that have been exposed between the upper strata and the rest. The idea that a liberal elite are entitled, by virtue of superior intelligence or educational attainment, to call the shots in all matters political, economic and social, was seen clearly in the aftermath of the Trump victory and Brexit. The controversy surrounding Brexit today exposes the full extent of the contempt of the elite for the rest. It is a highly dangerous development and a recipe for conflict and polarisation and perhaps even worse. The repercussions will not be confined to Britain alone. We should worry, when the wishes of 17.5 million voters, the majority of voters in the Brexit referendum, are ignored and the full force of the establishment, led by the BBC, are deployed to subvert the result. This is a serious undermining of democracy, which gives credibility to extreme views and fosters cynicism and hostility towards important institutions and values.

Social Cohesion

It would be very strange indeed if the arrival of almost one million foreigners, the equivalent of one quarter of the original population, did not have a huge effect on Irish society. The pretence that nothing has changed and everything is fine, is a classic 'elephant in the room' reaction, that seeks to deny the enormity of the event that has occurred. A tidal wave of migration has washed over the land, unique in the Western world in its length and intensity, bringing with it, not only huge numbers of people, but their sometimes conflicting values, culture, traditions and outlook.

Whether one is for or against, it should be accepted that this is a seismic event that warrants intense discussion and examination. It has changed the face of Ireland forever and will continue to change it into the future. The pretence that what has happened is without any drawbacks or difficulties belongs to the realm of fantasy. Seismic events such as this should always be discussed, even at the risk of being called a racist. After all, this is our country, our society, our culture and traditions.

Not only has this event delivered a huge demographic change but it has also shaken the structures and bonds in our society to the core, as seismic events invariable do. While the pro-migration lobby continually remind us of the enriching effects of diversity, nothing is ever said of the depleting effects. Chief among these is the corrosive effect of mass migration on the glue that holds our society together. That difficult to define feeling, that enables Irish people to salute those they do not know, is almost gone in most parts of Ireland. The fellow-feeling that allows the casual exchange of pleasantries with strangers, that once was the norm has been lost. It has been replaced by a constraint that has permeated society and chilled the atmosphere. This chilling process, is affecting the cohesion of our society, reducing the all-important levels of trust and cooperation.

While the sense of being part of a group that thinks the same way and shares an implicit understanding may be vague and subtle, it is the foundation of society. It is about the shared understanding that binds the group together and allows communities to form that are greater than the family or clan. Communities with shared ethnicity, language and culture, combine to form nations. The nation, no matter how primitive it may seem to the 'progressive' liberal individualist, is the ultimate collective human organisation. It inspires patriotism, loyalty and selflessness. Under its aegis great things can be achieved. Under its banner countless people have made the ultimate sacrifice and given their lives in defence of their way of life and their society.

The fellow-feeling of nationhood and community allow the immense task of building a civilised society to be undertaken. The willingness of individuals to put aside selfish interests and to make sacrifices for the common good, is the difference between civilisation and savagery. The idea of the nation galvanises and supports the collective effort and the trust required to share resources and to co-operate in great enterprises.

Sharing resources is never easy to do, even for the best of us. Yet the vast majority of us do it when we pay our taxes. We do it because a generally accepted consensus has decreed that important services are required for civilised living and these should be provided by the state and paid for by us. In making these undertakings we acknowledge the brotherhood of citizenship.

That concept of citizen brotherhood is not immune to change, events, erosion or even collapse. The advent of mass migration challenges the underlying bonds of ethnicity, culture, tradition and values. The vital but fragile implied understanding that permits societies to function is put at risk when large numbers of outsiders suddenly arrive, usually without an invitation and certainly without the assent of the majority. While people are prepared to share with their own in the spirit of national brotherhood, to expect them to include any number of uninvited strangers who take the notion to move to greener pastures, may well be a bridge too far.

One of the great creations of modern society is the welfare state. Painstaking efforts and sacrifices of past and present generations were required to build up the complex and expensive institutions and services that now constitute the generous Irish welfare state. This is not the property of some self-appointed elite to be disposed of as they see fit. The rapidly changing composition of the population is a direct threat to the feelings of solidarity, regard and trust essential to sustaining the benefits and obligations of the welfare state. No amount of wishful thinking or name-calling will change that.

The Clash of Cultures

Finding examples of the catastrophic consequences that follow when ethnic, religious or cultural groups clash is not difficult. We need look no further than Northern Ireland to see a classic example of deep-seated hatred, distrust, conflict and division in action. Even in its dormant state the jagged edges of suspicion prevent cooperation and agreement even on matters of common interest. But at least in Northern Ireland the factions have stopped killing each other.

In the 1990s a full-scale civil war erupted on European soil in Yugoslavia, with a death toll of 140,000 and enormous physical damage. This was an ethnic and religious conflict. In Eastern Ukraine today another ethnic conflict is taking place, again with much loss of life, destruction and population displacement. Europe itself is not immune from the ravages of open warfare and the presence of 78 million migrants (the UN figure for the whole of Europe in 2017)[5] could easily carry the seeds of future conflicts.

In Iraq, Syria and Yemen a religious war is being fought between Sunni and Shia aided and abetted by a sectarian line-up of neighbouring countries and their allies. The result has been a bloodbath and a massive displacement of people that threatens the stability of Europe. Similar ethnic, religious and cultural conflicts are taking place in Libya, Egypt, Somalia, Nigeria, Democratic Republic of Congo, Mali, Afghanistan, South Sudan and Turkey, to name but a few. These conflicts are generating a sizeable part of the influx of refugees and migrants into Europe. With the new arrivals, come their ethnic, religious and cultural baggage and rivalries, perhaps to be pursued in a new theatre of action on European soil. In addition, there are the inevitable tensions between migrants and the lower orders of natives with whom they are invariably billeted. It is very difficult to understand how any government or society could knowingly visit or encourage this scenario upon themselves, yet this is exactly what is happening in Europe today.

Racial tensions, riots, terrorism and unrest are now manifesting themselves in the West. Paris and the United States have seen racial riots recently. Terrorist attacks in Western Europe, emanating from districts populated by diverse ethnicities are a regular occurrence. Like the iceberg, this is the visible part of the problem, while just below the surface these tensions and unrest are bubbling away in the huge migrant enclaves of Europe's major cities.

This dark undercurrent is already a feature of life in Europe and in the foreseeable future this will intensify. The question of extent may depend on the flow of migrants into Europe. The alienation that breeds frustration, violence and crime is already here in abundance in the native underclass. If we allow a flood of migration to join them at the bottom of the social barrel, a stronger, more toxic cocktail is likely to result. Is there any merit in adding fuel to the fire by facilitating some 'progressive' borderless multicultural agenda and who exactly is going to benefit?

This cocktail of alienation and frustration will not be confined to the lower orders. Anything that erodes or dissolves the delicate mechanisms of social cohesion will be felt all across society. The existential challenge posed by mass migration to the welfare state – which is a vital part of the foundation of social cohesion here – is enormous. While reform is always necessary, the undermining of the social welfare system would seriously threaten the stability of Irish society. Unless migration is effectively controlled and considerably reduced, the ability of the taxpayer to maintain the present system will be fatally compromised, with unknown societal consequences.

10

The Law

We are living through a period of societal transformation and growing instability. There is a widespread sense of nervous foreboding about the future. Globalisation has not delivered the expected benefits for a large part of the population, in fact the opposite. Growing income disparity on the one hand and what appears to be increasingly fragile financial and economic systems in the West, coupled with austerity, are leading to disillusionment and restlessness in large parts of Western society. The problems of the shrinking purchasing power of wages and increasing costs that gave rise to the yellow vest movement in France, remains unresolved and is likely to spread into other developed countries. People are becoming polarised, with a looming clash in the offing between the liberal consensus establishment and a growing dissenting insurgency.

Meanwhile, in the developing world, much of the Middle-East has been ravaged by war, fuelled by sectarian hate and regional rivalry and facilitated by copious supplies of weapons. Hundreds of thousands have been killed and wounded and millions have been displaced. The contagion has spread into North and West Africa, bringing further instability and strife to these regions and unleashing further waves of migration. The numbers on the move are being augmented by an immense flood of economic migrants seeking the kind of lifestyles they see portrayed on Western media and the internet and escaping poverty and lack of opportunity at home. The cumulative result is a siege of Western Europe and other high-income regions by migrants from the developing countries. In societies where they have gained entry, enormous demographic and cultural upheaval has added to the unease and alienation of a large section of the native population.

Western Europe fails to protect its Borders

This cultural and demographic transformation will accelerate if the current lax migration policies and ineffective border controls continue to be implemented, adding to the anxiety and unease. For the moment, Turkey stands at the gates of Europe, holding back a flood of economic migrants and displaced and war-weary refugees. On Europe's southern flank, a much reduced stream of migrants from Africa and elsewhere are still putting to sea under the direction of a motley crew of people traffickers. The strategy of being towed out to international waters and waiting there for 'someone' to pick them up, which has been very effective, up to recently, while not entirely halted, is no longer viable. Before the Italian election in 2018, migrants were promptly deposited in Italian ports. This had been the case for a decade but had intensified over the last five years, trying Italian patience and helping to elect a large populist element to the Italian parliament. The government there had, until recently, been refusing to accept further migrants. A tug of war between NGOs, liberal sentiment and some Western European governments on the one hand and some Eastern European governments and many indigenous Europeans opposed to large scale migration on the other, continues. This is how Europe protects its borders!

While economic migration into Europe has slowed slightly, the problems that gave rise to it show no signs of abating. Poverty and lack of opportunity and rapid population growth continue to be widespread in the developing world. However, at the same time a considerable amount of economic growth is taking place and this is likely to provide the means to facilitate an increasing exodus. The next wave of migration into the developed world is now, more than likely, building up on its borders while awaiting the next opportunity to gain entry.

When considering this state of affairs, the first question to be asked is, should Europe be protecting its borders at all? From the point of view of the globalist, should everyone not be allowed to go wherever they please? This is a view held by a large section of society and an article of faith of politically correct ideology. It puts the rights of the individual, including free movement, before all else. Since this point of view, although not held by the majority, seems to dominate public discourse both here and in Europe, the dithering, incompetence and lack of resolve at official level, in tackling the border protection problem, plays right into this agenda. The aims of the pro-migration lobby continue to be achieved by default.

Europe has become the destination of choice for the countless millions of the underdeveloped world who want a better life. They know that if they go elsewhere they are more likely to be exploited and ill-treated. Japan or China do not have an immigration problem. Migrants know that if they get to Europe they will be fed, clothed and housed. They know that they will be immensely better off than they were at home. They also know that if they get here, it is very unlikely they will be deported. That is the reason why they come here to Europe and why they will continue to come.

Their desire for a better life is very understandable. However, the belief that somehow Europe should provide that 'better life' is simply wrong. There is no moral, ethical or legal basis to the argument that Europe owes a 'better life' to anyone other than Europeans. Would anyone argue that Nigeria owes a better life to Europeans, Chadians or the people of the Cameroon? Any kind of programme of structured or controlled migration into Europe - which is occasionally called for by pro-migration lobby groups and NGOs on the basis of offering a better life to the people of the developing world is fraught with the danger of enormous unintended consequences and must be rejected. As it stands, without any kind of programme, large numbers are coming to Europe each year.

If individual European countries decide to allow migration, as the Germans did in 2015 when they issued the Syrian invitation, they must be prepared to accept full responsibility for any and all of the consequences of their actions. Any attempt to unload part of the numbers that might respond, on their neighbours, is completely unacceptable. The unilateral action of the Germans in 2015 must never be repeated. Any such programme would be likely to unleash a monumental scramble to get in, that would dwarf the 2015 mass migration episode. It would also, more than likely, finally kill off the Schengen agreement if not the EU itself.

The failure to protect European borders is leading to a relatively rapid ethnic shift in the population of the Western part of the continent. The native peoples of this part of Europe have already been joined by tens of millions of migrants from the mainly poorer parts of the world. This is a process that has been in train for decades and is gaining momentum. It is evident in every large city in Western Europe today. In some places, like here in Ireland, it has spread not only to the cities but to the entire country, including remote rural parts. It is conceivable, if the process continues, that large parts of Europe will have non-native majorities within a generation or two, as has already happened in London.

It is not, at least for the moment, official government policy, nor is it the will of the people of Ireland or Europe to allow a situation to develop where Europeans are in a minority in their own countries. But, whatever the official policy, the fact is, that through incompetence and neglect, wilful or otherwise, Europe is rapidly being colonised by economic migrants and refugees from the developing world. The UN International Migration Report for 2017 informs us that in fifteen western European countries there are 54.4 million migrants, up 22 million from 2000, representing an average increase in immigrant numbers of 1.3 million a year.

Irish governments have continuously failed to join the dots between migration flows into Ireland and the growing housing, infrastructure and services problems. Irish electorates, misled and badly informed by a partisan pro-migration media, tolerate this situation because most of them are not fully aware of the extent of it. The public in general have, as previously mentioned, a great sympathy for the migrant. We do not seem to realise or care that our tolerance and sympathy are leading us into an act of collective national suicide. We cannot retain our identity, culture and traditions and put in jeopardy our economy and our services, if we allow what is effectively unlimited migration.

We are not alone in our failure to force our politicians to act on the migration issue. Little or nothing is being done to control the flow of migrants into Europe either. The wishes of the European public are being ignored. The Polish and Hungarian revolt against the EU Commission's insistence on taking in middle-Eastern refugees is a reflection of growing public resistance across Europe, particularly in the East, where government action and attitudes seem to better reflect public concerns. The emergence of anti-migration political parties in Holland, Austria, Germany, France, Denmark and Sweden also shows the resolve of the people of Western Europe to have their concerns acknowledged and their wishes respected.

The People Trafficking Industry

If Europeans want secure borders how can that be achieved? Surely not by outsourcing the job to the Turks for a fee or expecting a group of NGOs with their own agenda to do it. Frontex is the EU agency charged with protecting and controlling the borders of the Schengen area in conjunction with the various national police forces and it had a budget of €254 million in 2016 to do the job. While this may appear to be a lot of money it is nothing compared to the cost to European taxpayers of migration. Unsurprisingly, Frontex does not seem to be very effective. The people smuggling industry on the periphery of Europe, up to very recently, were running rings around the police and the border control agencies.

This racket was being indirectly sustained and encouraged by EU and NGO-backed activity in the Mediterranean. By all means, people in unseaworthy boats should be picked up and rescued from the sea, but they should be returned to the port from which their voyage originated. This seems to be happening to some extent now and it is the only way the problem of trafficking can be resolved. Suitable secure arrangements for accommodating these migrants should be made by the United Nations (UN) in conjunction with the local authorities at these ports and with the help of the 'regime change' coalition of France, Britain and the United States who must bear some responsibility for the destabilisation of Libya which greatly facilitated the trafficking business. The model for this already exists in other conflict zones. If necessary, safe havens should be established, policed and protected by the UN. The centres should be improved and developed to include work and educational opportunities for the residents. These centres should be supported financially by the rich countries including the EU and the Gulf States, as happens already in Turkey, Lebanon, Jordan and other parts of the Middle East. The cost of providing safe accommodation and facilities for migrants outside Europe, would be a fraction of what it costs European tax-payers to provide for them on European soil today.

Some of the people who have the means to pay people traffickers are not destitute. They are often from the middle-class and have the money to pay traffickers €5,000 to €30,000 for their services. They have decided, come what may, to move to Europe for a better life. Back in 1945, when De Valera, the then Irish Taoiseach, in reply to Churchill at the end of the War, famously said that he could not accept that *'Britain's necessity would become a moral code and that, when that necessity was sufficiently great, other people's rights were not to count'*, could equally be said of the migration situation today. Because people want a better life, they do not have the right or the moral justification to act illegally and enter other countries which they feel, can supply that need. This appears to be the new moral code behind migration. Real or perceived necessity cannot become the test for justifiable action.

Once an illegal migrant sets foot on European soil the authorities appear to lose control of the situation. UN conventions and the law are invoked to facilitate this form of illegal international travel and there appears to be nothing effective governments can do about it, short of withdrawing from the conventions. Growing numbers of bogus refugees and economic migrants are making their way to Europe every year. Once they get in, it is well-nigh impossible to get them to leave. Human rights lawyers have extended the grounds on which migrants and refugees can seek residency to such an extent that even the efficient Germans are overwhelmed. In 2015 when 1 million people arrived there, despite tougher rules, less than 20,000 were deported, just 2 per cent of the total. The Merkel invitation to Syrian refugees was seriously oversubscribed with economic migrants from elsewhere seeking a better life. Less than half the arrivals were Syrian, and yet, they came and they stayed.

The Germans are not alone in their failure to remove unwanted guests. Irish attempts at removal sometimes bordered on the farcical, as in the case of a Moroccan whose deportation was first ordered in 2009. This individual, according to a report in the *Sunday Times* on 14th July 2013[1], has cost the Irish taxpayer €700,000 in failed efforts to expel him. It also appears that he had been a guest of the Irish state (the taxpayer), for the four-year period prior to 2013. Did it not occur to the authorities to stop any payments by them to him? At that point two attempts had been made at deportation but each time, according to the report "he is said to engage in antisocial behaviour" when put on a flight. Gardaí abandoned a third attempt after he soiled himself as he was being placed on board a plane. This sounds woefully inept on the part of the authorities and calls into question their resolve and commitment to carry out this function with any degree of competence.

According to an ESRI report quoted in the *Sunday Times* 9 July 2017[2] only 20 per cent of deportation judgements are implemented. Failed asylum seekers continue to be accommodated, to hold medical cards, to access education and to receive exceptional needs payments from the Irish state, despite having deportation orders against them. Ireland is exceptional in this and the message it gives, is that the law can be treated with contempt. A review of parliamentary debates in the Dail indicated 'that the non-return of rejected applicants was not a focus'. The implication here is that our elected representatives have no regard for implementing the law in relation to illegal entry. In 2013 the High Court decided that the state had no power to enter a private dwelling to enforce a deportation order. Such is the legal and political shambles that surrounds the business of deportation in Ireland. **(See Appendix 7)**

The Irish authorities share this feeble approach to deportation with much of Europe. Frontex, the EU border agency, chartered a plane for €372,000 in December 2010[3] which broke down in Athens while deporting one hundred asylum seekers, 35 of whom were Nigerians from Ireland. These individuals were then sent back to Ireland, much to the satisfaction of refugee support groups here, who promised to reactivate the tortuous appeals processes for some of the cases.

The imagination, ingenuity and resolve of the people-smuggling industry is matched, if not exceeded, by the host of organisations dedicated to 'vindicating the rights' of illegal entrants once they arrive. An NGO (non-governmental organisation) claimed that 99 per cent of claims for *protection and giving leave to remain* are rejected, in an article in *The Irish Times* 17 December 2010[3]. This appears not to be the case, if the information given to John Perry TD (Fine Gael) on foot of a parliamentary question, tabled in November 2010, is correct, which says 34% of 6,356 of such claims were granted. In the period 2010 to 2013 724 failed asylum seekers and illegal immigrants were deported, at a cost to the Irish taxpayer of more than €2million, as reported in the *Sunday Times* on 21st July 2013[4]. Where are the other 3,500 that were rejected? The answer is that most of them, probably just disappeared into the woodwork. Others engaged in the long drawn out legal process of appeals and judicial reviews, at the taxpayer's expense, in a legal war of attrition. How many of the 70,000 refugee cohort that arrived before 2009 were deported? Probably very few if the German experience is anything to go by.

A thriving industry has grown up around the illegal entry phenomenon in Ireland. The Dublin Convention requires that asylum seekers register in the first country they enter after exiting the danger zone. Asylum is about safety from harm, not about choosing a venue to live the rest of your life that will live up to your expectations for a better life. This appears to be largely ignored by asylum applicants, who are acting illegally by ignoring the Dublin Convention and prefer to pick a favoured destination, instead of their first place of safety. A large number of NGOs, supported by generous wads of taxpayers' cash, doled out by our politicians, assist them in their efforts. The defendant and the bearer of all costs win or lose, is the Irish state – the taxpayer. The legal arm of the illegal entry business, spare no expense or effort, no matter how convoluted – it's all taxpayers' money anyway – in 'vindicating the rights' of their clients. In most cases they win, with the assistance of a very sympathetic judiciary and their client gets to stay.

An important decision, clarifying the criteria for judicial review of administrative decisions, was made by a three to two majority in the Irish Supreme Court in 2010. This opened up a legal and financial can of worms for the Irish taxpayer. It meant in practice, that every attempt to deport a failed asylum seeker would end up in the courts, according to dissenting Justice Hardiman in an article in *The Irish Times* 22 January 2010[5]. At one stroke, it superseded administrative procedures and decisions and made them subject to oversight and reversal by the courts. In doing so, it probably facilitated many bogus claims which would be difficult to disprove and had the added effect of clogging up the courts with judicial reviews. No doubt this has added another fruitful field of legal activity with rich pickings for some in the profession.

Not that the courts were not already clogged with dodgy asylum seeker cases. An unusual case, in that it ended in a deportation, was that of a financially and socially privileged Nigerian mother and her two children, dating back to 2005[6], as reported in an article in the *Sunday Times* on 3rd July 2011. A deportation order was issued in her case and she went into hiding but was later arrested. On release she applied for a judicial review and using, what the courts ultimately decided were forged documents, fought her case through the Irish courts all the way to the Supreme Court, at great expense to the Irish taxpayer. She led her supporters – which included celebrities, human-rights groups and politicians, including Mary Robinson, the former Irish President, the writer Roddy Doyle, the Fine Gael political party and Alan Shatter, who eventually had to deport her – a merry dance right through the entire legal system. Not satisfied with the Irish Supreme Court's decision, she appealed to the European Court of Human Rights who rejected the appeal in 2011.

This fiasco involved a government legal team that cost €370,000 and no fewer than five legal teams that represented herself and her two children at a cost of €700,000. Very few private citizens of this state could afford to indulge their passion for justice to this extent. How a non-Irish national, could illegally enter the state and proceed to expend large quantities of scarce public resources on an enterprise of doubtful merit, shows a serious disrespect, if not contempt for the tax-paying public. If, on the other hand, an Irish citizen, engaged in similar behaviour, surely they would be subject to severe sanction?

A worrying aspect of this case is that the Department of Justice said, at its conclusion – six years later in July 2011 – that it did not intend to reform the system to prevent this happening again. The taxpaying public are surely entitled to expect, that our legislators in Dail Eireann put in place a legal framework that deals efficiently and expeditiously with deportation cases and calls a halt to this costly legal shambles. Lessons should be learned from an experience, where gullibility and naivety may have led highly paid professionals in the courts, not to mention the celebrities, up the garden path. Reason and logic must outweigh what appeared to be emotional blackmail and lies in the courts.

A fertile field for emotional blackmail, that makes great media copy, is the area of 'the right to a family life' (Article 8 of the Human Rights Act). This has huge implications for Irish taxpayers and immigration. This principle can presumably be used by an individual who has secured residency in the state, to then bring in his or her family and then perhaps the extended family in an ever widening circle of entitlement. The 'right' to bring in dependants and family members exposes the taxpayer and the state to unsustainable levels of liability. A senior British expert in the field of migration, when writing about this issue, maintained that by 1997 migrants from low income countries were bringing in dependant relatives to such a considerable extent, that only 12 per cent of these migrants were actually coming to Britain to work[7]. This is an indication of how 'the right to a family life' can be used to unload economically inactive dependants onto another society, circumvent the rules and achieve unintended results as far as the host country is concerned. It also calls into question the much vaunted economic benefits of migration to the host country.

British courts have rejected the principle of automatic entitlement to bring in family members on certain grounds but it is probably only a matter of time, if it has not already happened, before case law and precedent establishes a de facto right. Hard cases make bad law but they are very effective at changing the law.

A new scam, whereby non-EU nationals with UK residency rights were attempting to bring in family members – under an EU directive sometimes referred to as the 'Surinder Sing rule'– from non-EU countries, was recently uncovered as described in an article on 2nd September 2018 in the *Sunday Times*[8]. These people would first move to Ireland from the UK, then bring their families to Ireland to obtain EU residency rights, before moving them back to Britain ahead of Brexit. These manoeuvres were organised by 'immigration advisers' in the UK, applying to the Irish authorities because the UK system was more 'stringent'. The practice was stopped. It says a lot about the ineffectiveness of Irish migration policy, when people were attempting to use an Irish backdoor to get around British rules.

Repatriation

While deportation falls into the category of forced repatriation, there are probably many situations where people would be prepared to return home voluntarily.

In a situation where large-scale migration is periodically taking place, the option of voluntary repatriation should be encouraged and made available to migrants, in certain circumstances. After the accession of new member states to the EU in 2004 and the extended large-scale immigration episode that followed, some of the new arrivals were unable to cope and ended up becoming homeless. The Department of Justice's Reception and Integration Agency ran a repatriation programme which was availed of by 348 EU nationals in 2006. It had been in operation from 2004. This programme should be revamped and extended to include some of the non-national homeless recently reported to be on Dublin's streets and indeed the many others who beg on streets all over the country or find it difficult to survive here. It could save the tax-payer a lot of money.

This scheme provided emergency accommodation followed by transport to an airport and a flight home. It was a humane solution for vulnerable people who were unable to adjust to new and often hostile circumstances in a foreign country. Family and local community support at home, is often preferable for those lacking the strong coping skills required in a highly competitive economic environment, like that prevailing in Ireland today. It is also the duty and the moral responsibility of their homeland, to provide for those who may not be able to fend for themselves.

The low skilled economic migrants who come here, are uniquely vulnerable to exploitation of all kinds. This is what so many employers love about them. They are willing to do almost anything for almost nothing. Many of these people, despite their willingness to work and their moderate expectations, find themselves struggling on the margins. They are often poorly housed, at exorbitant rent, presumably supplemented by the taxpayer. If they are working and many are not, their jobs are poorly paid and without security of tenure, which leaves them vulnerable to moneylenders. They do not have the pay levels or the permanency of employment to access the finance to establish themselves properly. In these circumstances, many would probably be better off at home, but they may lack the means to finance the trip.

This is where the Irish state should step in and provide a repatriation scheme which would cover travelling expenses and make a modest contribution to the cost of re-establishing them in their own country. The design of any such scheme would, of course, have to ensure that its clients would not return or encourage others to embark on a trip, with a view to taking advantage of Irish taxpayer generosity.

The French have run such a scheme where the average cost of voluntary repatriation has been about €2,500, which was very reasonable. The present Taoiseach, Leo Varadkar of Fine Gael, when in opposition, made a similar suggestion eleven years ago, as reported in the *Irish Independent* on 6 September 2008[9], to pay immigrant workers a lump sum payment of up to six months' worth of unemployment benefit, if they would agree to return home. He was immediately subjected to a torrent of indignant criticism led by the then Integration Minister Conor Lenihan and his Fianna Fail colleague Thomas Byrne, with a keen eye towards political point scoring. History soon vindicated Varadkar's approach, when, at the end of that very same month, the economy came crashing down. Within twelve months unemployment had risen from 240,217 to 419,854.

Had the Varadkar suggestion been acted upon it might have saved the Irish taxpayer a fortune. For migrants availing of it, there were also considerable benefits. In poor countries, the returning migrant would have had a reasonable capital sum at the end of the process. Compared to the cost of maintaining an unemployed migrant and their family in Ireland, on a permanent basis, this would have been a very good deal for Ireland too.

While a voluntary repatriation scheme could make a contribution to the problem of large-scale migration in Ireland, much else needs to be done. The uptake on such a scheme compared to the numbers already here and those arriving would probably be small. The generous levels of support provided by the Irish state through the taxpayer and the economic opportunities in an advanced society will always attract those who can finance the trip and are prepared to take the chance.

Criminality

An area where repatriation should be swift and free of the endless legal technicalities that often stand in the way of justice, is that of criminality. Globalisation should be delivering for the public in this area. Cooperation between police forces, law enforcement agencies and tax authorities should be taking place internationally and at all levels. Criminality should have no place to hide. Extradition on criminal charges should be largely a matter of form.

While this is happening to a certain extent, it is pathetically slow and inadequate compared to the vigour and intensity of the criminal organisations it is pitted against. Legal technicalities seem to hinder the law enforcement apparatus and allow criminality to treat society and its rules with contempt. In a recent case featured in the *Sunday Times* 18 March 2018, an Irish court refused to extradite an alleged Polish drug trafficker because it did not trust the Polish judicial system. Are Irish courts going to sit in judgement on the legal systems of other states, particularly other EU states, before extraditing alleged criminals[10]? The European arrest warrant system has been called into question by this action, impeding international law enforcement and providing solace and encouragement to criminals everywhere. To most people this looks like the judiciary inhibiting the ability of society to come to grips with lawlessness.

Globalisation, instead of helping in the fight against criminality, has facilitated the growth and operations of multinational criminal organisations by reducing or eliminating border checks, allowing virtual free movement of people, some of whom are criminals, as well as capital, goods and services and failing to monitor and control adequately the arms trade. Free movement is also facilitating the illegal drugs trade which is now so rich and powerful that it can prosecute its own wars and threaten the sovereignty and stability of some of the states where it operates. The proceeds of all these criminal activities can be quickly transferred from one jurisdiction to another and laundered in an almost frictionless global financial system.

People-trafficking is another growing international criminal enterprise, potentially larger and more destabilising than the drugs trade. Its possible client base is numbered in tens of millions. It has been estimated that world-wide there are as many as 40 million slaves, many of whom have been trafficked. The victims of trafficking also include those desperate, terrified people fleeing war, as well as the seekers of a better life, the adventurous, the ambitious and the disillusioned, who use these services that are invariably costly, dangerous and unreliable. The other victims of this modern scourge are Western societies and their taxpayers, who must pick up the tab for illegal migration and all the housing, welfare, medical, educational and legal costs involved.

While it might have been expected that a more integrated, globalised approach to policing the people trafficking epidemic would have emerged by now, the opposite appears to have happened. The Merkel invitation has acted as a massive boost for the traffickers, by encouraging many who would otherwise have stayed where they were, to avail of their services. The migration agreement between the EU and Turkey has put a temporary, partial brake on the problem in the eastern Mediterranean. But, since the initially hopeful Arab Spring turned sour, arguably worsened by outside meddling, the EU has stood aside as tribal and civil strife spread into Libya. Undercover of this lawlessness, the traffickers diligently go about their business without let or hindrance. The same resolve and resources must be applied to this problem as would be applied to a major financial or political crisis. As things stand, the future of the EU itself has been compromised by the ongoing migration shambles, in part at least, facilitated by human trafficking.

People trafficking is just one aspect of criminality associated with migration. Another major cause for concern is the number of foreign criminals on the move internationally and within the EU. Some of these are coming to Ireland under EU freedom of movement rules and end up in Irish prisons. One quarter of the inmates of Irish prisons in 2004 were foreigners although the non-national population at the time was less than 10 per cent. This was comprised of 2,520 individuals from 115 countries, according to an article in *The Irish Times* on 22 December 2004[11]. As if we haven't enough criminals of our own, Romanian, Polish, Latvian, Russian, Nigerian and Chinese gangs are now operating here and have been linked to organised prostitution, contraband smuggling, weapons, drugs, people and child trafficking. Vietnamese human slaves are extensively used in cannabis grow-houses run by criminal gangs in Ireland. Strong growth in the demand for the services of sex workers in the Celtic Tiger period, led to large numbers of women being trafficked into the country from Eastern Europe, Africa and Asia. In 2013 the Gardaí said foreign nationals are now central players in the Irish underworld.

With 50,000 to 60,000 non-national migrants arriving here every year, the job of identifying and monitoring criminal elements is difficult. The use of technology, DNA sampling and other data should be playing an important role here but is being frustrated by squeamishness about civil rights infringement. It may take a terrorist attack to change people's minds about the necessity for this. The gardaí were criticised by the Data Protection Commissioner for integrating the fingerprints of asylum seekers with normal criminals in an audit in 2014 according to the *Sunday Times* on 13 April 2014[12]. The garda exercise led to the identification of one of the most wanted people in Europe, who turned up as a Nigerian asylum seeker in Dublin. He was later extradited to Holland and convicted of being involved in trafficking up to 100 children and 150 women into Europe. The Dutch prosecutor cited the garda police work as a good example of how police forces in the EU can work together.

The hair-splitting in relation to data, that led to the criticism of the gardaí is an impediment to efficient policing and potentially puts the public at risk. The key to combating the growing threat of terrorism and increasingly sophisticated criminality is integrating data from all possible sources. If there is a clash with data protection and the freedom of the individual on the one hand and the public good on the other, it is up to Dail Eireann to clarify the situation, giving appropriate weight to the interests of the common good.

The freedom of movement of the individual is an article of faith of the EU. This principle also appears to apply to the criminal fraternity. While the US and others will not allow individuals with criminal convictions to enter their territory, we in Ireland are prepared to admit criminals not just from the EU but from other places as well. Denis Naughten TD (Fine Gael at the time), in commenting on two convictions for murder by two immigrants with criminal records, in the *Irish Independent* on 28 January 2008[13], said *'the Dept. of Justice should refuse entry to those who have been involved in serious criminal activity. Those convicted of serious offences by the Irish Courts should also be deported'.* This sounds very reasonable and would be supported by most people.

Whatever Naughten and the rest of the country thought, our masters in Brussels and their minions here had different ideas. Charlie Flanagan TD, then justice spokesman for Fine Gael and now Justice Minister, put forward the excuse that *'it was not possible to build a "fortress" where people with criminal records were blocked from entering the state'.* Try telling that to Homeland Security in the United States. This is just not good enough. Many things are not possible when the will and resolve to do them are lacking.

The question of excluding and deporting criminals seeking to enter the state is about the sovereignty of the state and its duty to protect its citizens. No government worth its salt should allow foreign criminals to enter their territory and should deport foreigners convicted in their courts, as Deputy Naughten rightly said. Some of us would like to see this proposition added to the list of issues in the 'progressive referenda' pipeline. The contention that foreign criminals somehow have a right to free movement, as implied by Charlie Flanagan's comment, belongs to the PC compendium of ideological nonsense.

Under the guise of defending the rights and freedoms of the individual, Irish, European and international law appear to have banded together to subvert the interests of the common good. Using exceptional, bizarre or particularly hard cases, precedents are being set which drive a coach and four through the common sense approach to formulating the rules and regulations that are needed to assist in the conduct of human affairs in a fair, just and equitable fashion. The unintended consequence of some of these legal developments, is that a wide range of international criminal activity, from people trafficking and modern slavery to the arms and drugs trade, far from being impeded, are being assisted and facilitated.

11

The Allure of a Better Life

The United Nations International Migration Report 2017 estimated that there were 258 million migrants − people living in countries other than the ones they were born in − up 85 million or nearly 50 per cent from 2000 figure. This presumably does not include the children they have produced in the intervening time, who were born in their new country of residence. If that trend were to continue for the next sixteen years and all the other factors remained stable, the number of migrants could be around the 400 million mark by 2033 which, if their children are included, could double that number. The problem for Europe and North America is that migration naturally gravitates toward high income countries like those of the West, where access is relatively easy, the social protection system can be availed of, the rule of law prevails and crucially, standards of living are far higher than where they have come from.

The High Income Migration Magnet

The destination of choice in the future, as now, for those who migrate will be high income Western countries. While this is all very understandable from the migrant point of view, for some of us at least, it's a bit like having a large number of uninvited, poverty stricken guests in your own home, who have been directed to your residence by a friendly UN official who has assured them that you will not mind and in fact, it will be good for you. This is hardly a satisfactory situation. There are just so many chores you can ask them to do in recompense for the lodging. When a certain point is reached and they have settled in for the long haul, you will find that your house is no longer your own.

Unless we in the West decide to protect our borders and rigorously control and greatly reduce immigration, we will end up with a huge number of people from the developing world, to be accommodated, to find employment for, to educate their children and to look after their health. With more globalisation, easier faster travel, more technology and internet access and more financial resources, the people of the developing world have become more mobile than ever. With an overwhelming desire for a better life, whetted by television, advertising and the internet, the likelihood is that the desire to migrate, will not only continue, but will accelerate substantially.

In high income countries like those of Western Europe, the United States, Canada and Australia the number of migrants as a proportion of the population is now 14.1 per cent, while in the rest of the world it's less than 2 per cent *(UN Migration Report 2017)*[1].

If we continue as we are, the question for Europeans and Ireland then becomes, how many will come here? The sixteen principal countries of Western Europe, including Ireland, are already hosting 54.7 million migrants *(UN Migration Report 2017)* – not including their children – up nearly 70 per cent from 2000. If the current trend were to continue, a 70 per cent increase in the next sixteen years would deliver another 38 million to those sixteen countries. It is probably optimistic – if that's the right word

– to think that the current trend will just be maintained. The strong economic growth in the developing countries today will provide the financial resources to more people to migrate, facilitating the movement of even larger numbers into Western Europe.

Already more than 13 per cent of the population of these countries are migrants. In Ireland we are way ahead of the average with migration accounting for 17 per cent of our population in 2016 *(the UN Migration Report 2017)* and rising at more than half a per cent a year. While the Irish people appear to be unperturbed by this situation, there is much concern all over Europe about demographic change. This concern is having a profound effect on European politics and is driving the populist challenge to the European political establishment. At some point in the future, we can expect these concerns to emerge in Ireland also.

The UN Backs Migration

To the liberal consensus leaders who still hold the levers of power in most of Europe, this is a worrying development. Nevertheless, they persist with the same migration policies that operated before the populist revolt, with minor adjustments. These policies unsurprisingly, are also in accord with the 2017 Report of the UN Under-Secretary-General for Economic and Social Affairs Wu Hongbo, who said *'Well managed migration brings important benefits to countries of origin and destination'*. Certainly for the countries of origin it brought considerable benefits in the form of $413 billion in remittances, which presumably was a loss to the economies of the host countries. On the question of well managed migration, 'well managed' is not a term usually associated with recent migration, in the minds of the European public, where visions of the 2015 German mass migration episode come to mind. The only country in Europe that had the opportunity to pass judgement on the benefits of migration – Britain – rejected this point of view.

The UN report went on to list the benefits to the 'countries of destination' which, depending on your point of view, might or might not be described as such. The first one was 'filling critical labour gaps', which is very useful to employers who want to avoid the bother or expense of training indigenous labour or indeed, of paying competitive rates. It also has the added bonus of providing opportunities for migrant exploitation. One might also ask, in the European context, what critical labour gaps? There were 16.8 million unemployed workers in the EU (in 2018), not including those on work schemes. From the taxpayer perspective the use of migrant labour has the disadvantage of having the native population on the dole, which can be a substantial social welfare cost. Migrants who fill labour gaps may also require housing, health, education and infrastructural services which will be a burden on the state in many cases.

Another contribution listed by the UN is that migrants, as entrepreneurs, may create jobs, which is excellent if they do. However, the experience in Ireland is that if migrants are successful in business, many of them import their own labour, usually their family or friends.

The UN says that migrants pay taxes and social security and of course that is as it should be. The problem in Ireland is that not all do and in many cases through no fault of their own. Unscrupulous employers often employ migrants in black economy operations that exploit the migrants and defraud the state, and the very fact that they are migrants facilitates this type of crime.

While migrants who work generally do pay taxes, the public have no idea how many migrants arrive here and do not work at all. This important information does not appear to be readily available, perhaps because it might shed some unfavourable light on the anomalies in the labour market and its interface with the social welfare system and indeed, on the wider question of the disadvantages and costs of migration to the host country. Part of the lack of transparency in relation to migrant dependence on social welfare, is the view that it might lead to hostility or racism. Unfortunately, human existence is always vulnerable to hostility and unpleasantness. Notwithstanding, taxpayers are entitled to know, in every detail, what their money is being spent on.

Another benefit of migration to the host nation, in the eyes of the UN, is that migrants can be 'dynamic members of the host society'. How many people should be given access, to yield a handful of 'dynamic individuals'? This sounds like a doubtful sales pitch with little substance, that might nevertheless be true in exceptional cases but it is hardly grounds for allowing access to a country. Not many people will bring what the Clancy Brothers brought to New York in the 1960s or what Tony O'Reilly brought to corporate America.

'Cultural diversity' is another UN hard-to-define benefit that may not appeal to those who have to pick up the bill, if there is a cost involved. Not everyone likes Chinese, Indian, Italian or Sushi restaurants and Turkish barbers. The question will be asked, how many exponents of cultural diversity do we need?

Finally, the UN thinks that migrants can contribute to the development of science and technology, which is undoubtedly true. However, for migrants from poorer countries, the application of science and technology to the problems in their own countries, would, in general, be a much better and worthwhile application of their talents.

The UN says that migration is here to stay – presumably in ever increasing amounts – and that we need to get used to it. Migration, of course, was always here but never, until recent times, in such gargantuan amounts. Most people agree that a certain amount of migration is necessary and desirable. But what we have today, which many do not agree with, is mass migration, where the numbers arriving have a significant and not always benign impact on the native populations. The UN, as a globalist organisation, may see itself in the role of global regulator on a number of fronts, with an increasingly important role in world affairs. As is the nature of such organisations, there seems to be a genetic imperative to extend their remit into every area and activity possible. When such a bureaucracy reaches a critical mass, it reproduces itself automatically and not always to the benefit of its members. We have seen a similar process unfold in regard to the EU, where the servant becomes the master.

The enabling role of the UN in relation to mass migration has been critical. The ability of sovereign states to control their borders has been fatally compromised by various UN conventions. The migration lobby and the human rights industry have constructed a legal freeway in relation to migration, on the basis of UN conventions. The 'United' in the UN title is possibly seen as a mission to demolish borders and effectively that is what it is doing. While in theory it may be acting on the authority of its members in this regard, it is not acting on the authority of their electorates.

The vast majority of migrants today are economic migrants. The vast majority of refugees eventually become economic migrants, when the requirement for refuge and protection ends and they invariably remain in whatever location they have managed to reach.

Mass migration for economic reasons should not be happening in the twenty-first century. In a world where capital moves freely, at the touch of a button, capital should move to places where labour abounds, not the other way around. The UN should be promoting capital migration, not facilitating the movement people around the world with all the seen and unforeseen consequences that may ensue, many of them negative. That could involve the UN calling places like Ireland, Switzerland, Jersey, Luxembourg and a host of off-shore tax havens and a whole network of tax scammers, banks, financial institutions and wealthy individuals to order, for manipulating financial rules unfairly and thereby causing economic and social chaos.

Does the liberal mind-set seriously believe that the mass migration of poor people to rich countries can solve the developing countries' poverty problems? If this is the best that liberalism can offer in terms of a solution to the poverty question, then it shows the bankruptcy of its ideas. The pre-eminence of the individual and their freedom of movement in liberal thinking offers a solution to a handful, relatively speaking, of talented, ambitious or desperate individuals while the destitute billions must stay put and fend for themselves.

The Brain Drain

Migration may solve a problem for those individuals who can move but it creates at least three other problems. The first and most important is the loss of the individual and their talents to the country of origin. The second is, if the individual finds work in a new country, he or she shifts their poverty onto the indigenous poor of the host country by gaining employment to their exclusion. And the third is, if they fail to find work, then the burden falls back on the native taxpayers' welfare system.

An example of this kind of scenario in action is the Irish Health Service Executive (HSE) recruitment policy. The HSE has hired a number of doctors from South Sudan. This is a country of 11 million people where a civil war has taken place and may be continuing, with 400,000 war-related deaths. Many of its people have been displaced and poverty, disease and starvation are widespread. This is a country that needs doctors urgently − far more urgently than Ireland, despite our GP shortage. Yet, the Irish health service is recruiting some of its doctors, who are very expensive to train, from one of the poorest countries in the world.

The Royal College of Surgeons in Ireland says this is in contravention of Ireland's responsibility not to recruit doctors from poorer countries. At the moment there are 1,481 Pakistani and about half that number of Sudanese doctors here, as stated in an article in *The Irish Times* on 22 June 2017[2], who are badly needed at home. Similarly, many of the 725 doctors we trained ourselves in 2015, at enormous expense to the Irish taxpayer and with little regard for any obligation to their own society, migrate to better paying locations.

This is the other side of the migration story and a stark example of the individualism at the heart of liberal thinking. A relatively wealthy country like Ireland is stealing from one of the poorest and most needy places on the planet. Extremely scarce resources have been invested in training badly needed medical personnel, only to have them poached by outsiders with bigger cheque books. This is the global market at work.

The poor countries from which most migrants come, invest large parts of their meagre resources in education. Many of their brightest and best students, having partaken of the best education their communities struggle and sacrifice to provide, migrate to the greener pastures of the developed world, where salaries and lifestyles are better. Their native land has wasted its resources and lost an individual who would make an important contribution to their community.

The 'brain drain' is an important factor impeding the progress of poorer countries. The loss of the well-educated and the skilled can affect society on a number of levels. The development and reform of political, social and economic structures in poorer countries should be the business of their brightest and best. Instead, they are all too often engaged in forging careers in the developed world, where their talents – while better paid – may not be appreciated or needed to the same extent.

From the point of view of some of these well-educated and skilled individuals, it is obviously too much to ask that they should forego some material advantage and partake in the process of nation building at home. Weak national identity – the bête noire of the liberal elite in the West – can be a factor inhibiting the enormous efforts required to create a successful society. The self-sacrifice that is part of the price of progress will not be undertaken when the first loyalty is to the tribe, the clan or the extended family. National pride and patriotism transcends petty squabbles and differences and personal agendas in the successful society. Apart altogether from patriotism, there is a certain moral obligation on those who have had the privilege of drinking deeply at the well of knowledge, to assist those who made it possible.

If poor countries are ever to prosper, the stranglehold of the extractive elites who often govern them must be broken. This is not easily done. The people best equipped to provide the leadership and often the selfless actions required to bring this about, are often the ones who migrate. Revolution, struggle and turmoil over the last 300 years, eventually wrested some of the power from the same extractive elites in Europe and America. The structures and laws that hold these forces in check must be created, maintained and renewed as required, something which we in the West still struggle to do. Real progress, change and reform are a process that require blood, sweat and tears and cannot usually be achieved at a safe distance in some developed economy.

The shameful spectacle of Western leaders trooping over to the glittering courts of the Middle East with their entourages of arms dealers, touting for billion dollar sales deals is an affront to civilisation and common sense. This reckless behaviour, often characterised by its participants as job creation schemes for European and American workers, is relentlessly pushing the Middle East towards a major conflict between Saudi Arabia and its Sunni allies and Iran and its Shia supporters, with untold consequences for the region and indeed the entire world. This is one of the main reasons for the destabilisation of the Middle East and North Africa and a key factor driving large-scale migration from these regions. To the educated and skilled, who should be leading the push for reform and progress at home, the flood of arms and the resulting violence and instability is the last straw. Instead of building harmonious societies, they want to leave, and who could blame them?

The tragedy for war-torn, unstable and poorer countries is that their most valuable citizens, those who are most economically active, are also the most mobile. The middle-class, professionals, the educated and the skilled often have the considerable resources required to finance a legal or illegal exit. People traffickers cost money. The poor, the destitute and vulnerable, just cannot afford the fare.

The practice of granting access to skilled workers and graduates by some developed countries is often held up as a 'progressive' migration policy. For the country of origin it is an act of economic piracy, draining a limited pool of badly needed talent and energy. It is, in fact, just another self-serving ploy, to plug gaps in the labour market on the cheap, at the expense of the poor countries that have educated and trained these individuals. Instead of providing education and apprenticeships for locals, it's cheaper for business to import them, preferably at a discount. The market cares nothing for social obligations or unforeseen repercussions.

The Brawn Drain

However, despite all the obstacles, significant growth is taking place in many of the poorer countries and with that growth comes mobility. Not only are the educated and skilled on the move, which was always the case, but an increasing number of young less skilled migrants are adding volume to the exodus. This new element is putting the volume into mass migration. They are not from the bottom billion but the tier just above. These are the boat people from Libya and the millions of others, who are now attempting to gain access to Europe. With greater income and savings, improving infrastructure and transport, there will be many more in the future. The precedent set by the Merkel invitation will not be lost on the possible billion or so people in the developing world, who feel sure they would be far better off in the developed world but do not yet have the means to make the trip.

Environmental deterioration, whether man-made or natural, on the perimeters of the great deserts, together with prolonged droughts, are already adding to the numbers on the move. The population explosion is continuing unabated in many of the poorer countries, with Africa leading the way, despite its economic growth. The Indian sub-continent, vulnerable to rising sea levels, is another population hot spot, where the huge numbers already living there are swelling at an alarming rate, despite the economic growth which tends to moderate birth rates. Population growth, on its own, has the potential to set off a catastrophic tsunami of migration. The wonder surely is – that it has not already happened.

Every landslide needs a catalyst. The migration landslide in Germany in 2015 was triggered by the German response to the Syrian conflict but less than half of those who migrated were victims of the war. The wars in Syria, Iraq, Libya, Congo and Afghanistan and new outbreaks in Yemen, Somalia, Nigeria, Mali and South Sudan, may well provide the catalyst for the next landslide. The conditions are ripe for a further mass exodus, possibly a lot larger than the last.

In the medium to long term, if the grinding poverty, political instability, war, famine and disease persist in the poorer countries, their inhabitants will increasingly turn up at our door looking for assistance and brandishing the UN Declaration of Human Rights. The German influx of 2015 was coordinated by social media, the internet and technology. They are the tools that are likely to play a key role in future migration episodes. Breaches or weaknesses in European borders are likely to be quickly notified to interested parties. Many migrants have extensive knowledge of international law and human rights legislation and what they lack will be provided by a host of helpful NGOs in the receiving countries. They assess their chances of success against the prevailing conditions and up to now the vast majority have succeed in staying if they make it to European soil. The legal framework is already in place, through various UN declarations, to oblige us to render whatever assistance is required and this will undoubtedly include admitting unprecedented numbers of refugees and migrants in the future. For Europe, in the medium to long term, this could mean tens, if not hundreds of millions, of which Ireland would have to take its share.

FTT – the New Marshall Plan

If we continue to trust the markets to resolve the economic problems of the human race we may find that the poverty-stricken majority take matters into their own hands and decide, by sheer force of numbers and desperation, to take their share regardless of rules and regulations. This is what happened when the workers of the nineteenth and twentieth century, through industrial action, wrested a share of the wealth they created from the reluctant capitalists of the time. It was a bitter and damaging struggle.

We in the West must also face up to the global problem of assisting the developing countries in the mammoth task of providing their people with decent living standards or face the consequences. Those consequences are already manifesting themselves on our borders in the form of mass migration.

There can be no underestimating the magnitude of this task. What is required, is that the economies of the poorer countries be rapidly developed to provide jobs and incomes to sustain civilised living for the populations of those countries, just as the Chinese are doing today in their own economy. To achieve this, massive resources must be deployed, of the same scale and magnitude as those mobilised to counteract the global financial meltdown of 2008. The EU alone spent €4.6 trillion of taxpayer's money, up to mid-2012[3], propping up the financial sector, not to mention what was spent in the United States and elsewhere. If we can harness the same commitment, energy and resources with which the financial crisis was tackled, we can solve this problem too.

The financial burden to be shouldered in this enterprise, if we decide to undertake it, should be borne to the greatest extent by those who benefited most by globalisation, the rich and the super-rich, who own an ever increasing share of the world's wealth and not the ordinary taxpayer who paid for the financial crisis of 2008. The European Commission proposed a Financial Transaction Tax (FTT) after the 2008 crash, of 0.01% on the sale of financial instruments, much like VAT (which is not charged on these sales), but a whole lot less. This would be paid by the financial services sector and presumably passed on to their clients, who deal in these financial instruments. Almost the first out of the trenches and into the fray in opposition to this very modest proposal was liberal Ireland. They opposed it at both European Commission and Parliament level, in line with their consistently strong defence of the rich at all times.

If globalisation is anything other than a means by which the rich get richer, then a global Financial Transaction Tax (FTT) should be agreed at the UN and not just the EU, just like the Paris Climate Change agreement, only more effectively enforced. The fund created could be used to tackle economic equality for poorer countries, population stabilisation, climate change, natural disasters when they occur and other global issues. The rate of the tax as suggested by the European Commission at 0.01% was miniscule, compared to what European workers' pay in income taxes and should be increased by at least a factor of fifty, to effectively combat these problems. This would also help to address global environmental issues more holistically and effectively, while avoiding transferring the burden onto the shoulders of the poor.

If we believe in equality let's call out Liberal Ireland on the FTT, even if it hurts their wealthy friends a little. Of course there would be objectors and from past experience it is clear Ireland would be one of the first. The operations of the network of off-shore and on-shore tax havens – including Ireland – would have to be shut down and replaced by global financial transparency. Global economic and financial solidarity should ensure that pockets of resistance could be persuaded in time by the achievements of the fund, but if all else fails, these objectors could be sanctioned or excluded from the economic, social and cultural life of the complying world community.

A Catalogue of Errors

As I have been attempting to discuss in this book, the negative effects of mass migration on the economic, social and cultural life of the bottom half of Irish society in particular, has been substantial. The spectacular implosion of the Celtic Tiger was the inevitable result of policies that had allowed the economy to spiral out of control. This happened because the political establishment, from right to left, the business elite and the trade unions, embraced a consensus view that allowed market forces and light regulation to run amok. In the 1990s when cheap money and cheap labour flooded into the country and turbocharged the economy, nobody shouted stop. Nobody even seemed to notice. The granting of unfettered access to the eastern European states in 2004 gave a further massive boost to an already overheated economy and ensured a catastrophic crash landing. A key element in the Celtic Tiger phenomenon and the difference between it and previous economic cycles was mass migration, which, as Goodbody Stockbrokers said *'boosted the supply and demand sides of the economy'*– to melting point. Nowhere was this more evident than in the construction sector, which ballooned to totally unsustainable heights before collapsing, dragging down the rest of the economy in its wake.

It was an economic catastrophe of the first order which has had a devastating effect on the lives of the less well off. Income and living standards plummeted and unemployment, taxation and debt levels rose significantly. The enormous weight of mass unemployment, which was augmented by the high levels of inward migration, weighed heavily on the social welfare structure. These factors and migrant competition in the labour market, continue to exert significant downward pressure on living conditions for the less well off.

On the social side, the housing crisis we are experiencing today is a direct result of the influx that has been ramping up over the last five years, intensifying demand for accommodation in a tight market. Migration is bringing about circumstances which may eventually lead to a situation where, particularly the less well-off will no longer be able to afford a house of their own. This has very detrimental implications for the individuals themselves, in terms of continuously rising rents, insecurity of tenure and the frustration of legitimate home ownership aspirations. It also has vast implications for the taxpaying public who will have to shoulder the burden of providing social housing for a growing proportion of the population.

Another social side effect of mass migration is the deterioration of the health and education services. Access to even basic health services like the general practitioner are now becoming increasingly difficult and access to hospital and consultant services for those relying on the public health service are subject to unacceptable delays. The migrant population is concentrated in the bottom half of society and are unlikely to have private health insurance, so their presence is adding to the strain on the public health service. School places for young children have also become problematic in some areas, due to increased demand. With one quarter of the school-going population of migrant origin, this must be having a massive bearing on access to school places.

If the numbers of migrants entering the state continue at the present levels or escalate, the Irish welfare state will inevitably become unsustainable. Already half of the residents in the country are receiving payments from the state. Even in a full employment situation many working migrants and our own indigenous working poor are dependent on the state to some extent, through supplementary benefits, children's allowance and subsidised rents. When the next economic downturn occurs we could find ourselves in a similar situation to the Greeks today, where welfare must be cut savagely.

Culture and Identity are Precious

While the economic and social aspects of mass migration are of enormous importance, they are not the only issues of consequence. In terms of culture and identity there is a huge amount to be lost if the diversity of National identities is overwhelmed by economic migration. Just like preserving our biodiversity – our snails, wild birds, or animals – so it is with the cultural diversity of nations. Do we want to see Irish or European culture become a side-show, confined to a series of Disney-land-like theme parks, surrounded by a surging, churning mass of humanity, driven by economic necessity from one hub of activity to another at the whim of the market and indistinguishable from one end of the globe to the other? Will the last ethnic Europeans live out their lives on reservations in the foothills of the Urals in 500 years' time, like the native peoples of North America do today? Perhaps these considerations should not concern us − perhaps they are none of our business? And yet they are the very issues that convulse public discourse in the West today.

There are enormous benefits to be derived from global cooperation on economic, financial, scientific, environmental and other areas but the annihilation of cultural and national identities is not one of them. The world was horrified by the destruction of Palmyra. We should be equally aghast at any attempt to dismantle the cultural heritage of nations and the borders that help to protect them.

The abject poverty of a third of humanity is as dangerous a threat to stability and peace as nuclear war or global warming. It will not be solved by the mass migration of the poor to the rich countries. It need not lead, like the great depression of the 1930s, to a world war. The developed countries need to provide whatever financial resources and technical and managerial skills are required, to assist in the development of the poorer countries in a new Marshall-type plan.

Whatever the cost, the closely related global problems of poverty, war, environmental degradation, over population and mass migration, must be tackled with great urgency. Time is running out. The alternative for Europeans − and they could be the biggest losers − is a repeat, in cultural, social and economic terms, of the fall of the Roman Empire, submerged, not by barbarian hordes from the East but by economic migration from the South. This time there will be no 'Island of Saints and Scholars' where European identity, heritage and culture are preserved. This time Ireland will be at the forefront of the invasion and unlike the Norman Conquest or British colonialism, it will entail the obliteration of that unique Irish identity and vision. It has not only started, it is already well advanced.

Notes

Introduction

1. Article in The Irish Times 9th January 2016 by Breda O'Brien 'Finns could teach us a lesson on diversity in political discourse'.

1   The Demographic Shift

1. UN World Population Prospects Report 2017
2. CSO Press Statement (April 2017) Census 2016 Summary Results – Part 1. Highlights of the report.
3. UN International Migration Report 2017: Highlights (page28)
4. CSO (Central Statistics Office) Press Statement 27th August 2019 'Population and Migration Estimates 2019'.
5. Article in The Irish Times on 20th November 2013 by Carl O'Brien
6. Article in The Sunday Business Post on 6-7th January 2019 (pages 1 and 2) by Jack Horgan-Jones and Ian Guider 'Work permits backlog "hitting ability to attract foreign investment"'.
7. Article in The Irish Times on 15th July 2017 by Patrick Freyne 'Unknown unequal undone'.
8. See article in the Sunday Times on 20th September 2015 by Bojan Pancevski '"Moral" Germany cracks as the world turns up on its doorstep'.

2   Political Correctness and the Liberal Consensus

1. See article in the Irish Times on 22nd September 2017 by Carl O'Brien 'Irish workers the most over qualified in Europe for the jobs they have'.
2. Article in the Sunday Times 27th May 2018 by Larissa Nolan

3   The Left Looses the Plot

1. Article in the Sunday Business Post 30th June 2002 by Sean Mac Carthaigh 'Immigrants from new EU states set to flock to Ireland' (page 1) and 'Ireland to allow access to foreign workers' (page 2)
2. Letter from David Begg in relation to unfettered access to the Irish Labour Market
3. Article in the Irish Independent 26th November 2005 by Senan Moloney and Ralph Riegel 'Industrial showdown looms as row places social partnership in danger'
4. Article in the Irish Independent 31st October 2005 by Helen Bruce 'New employment laws will bring flood of cheap labour, warns Siptu'.
5. Article in the Irish Independent on the 15th September 2000 by Pat Boyle 'Workers fail to cash in on the boom: ESRI report'
6. Article in the Irish Independent 14th February 2004 by Willy Dillon 'Invasion of the job snatchers? Not likely?'
7. Article in the Irish Independent on the 27th February by Conor Sweeney 'EU enlargement fears are unfounded, survey finds'.
8. Article in the Irish Independent May 2004 by Nigel Morris and Stephen Castle 'Britain to curb benefits for new EU immigrants'.
9. See article in the Irish Independent on 23rd March 2004 by Pat Boyle 'Enlargement will lead to greater unemployment, claims new report'.
10. Article in the Irish Independent 24th January 2006 by Brian Dowling 'What we need by 2016...300,000 more'.

4 The Irish Klondike

1. Article in the Irish Independent on 4th April 2004 by Martin Fitzpatrick 'Harney's riled by top tax man's jibe over Irish rates'.
2. Article in the Irish Independent 2nd April 2005 by Paul Melia '"Flood" of migrant workers proves a fantasy'.
3. Article in the Irish Independent 23rd March 2006 by Brendan Keenan and Edel Kennedy 'Through the roof'.

4. Article in the Sunday Independent 8th February 2009 by Ronald Quinlan 'Immigrants not factored into job loss estimates'.

5. Central Statistics Office Press Statement 27th August 2019 Population and Migration Estimates April 2019.

6. Article in the Sunday Times 2nd September 2007 by Stephen O'Brien 'Migration "far higher than stated"'.

7. Article in the Irish Independent 1st November 2007 by AilishO'Hora 'New Irish now account for 17pc of workforce'

8. Article in the Sunday Times 7th April 2013 by Melanie McDonagh 'Oops, we try to outsmart Germany and end up with a wave of Bulgarians'.

9. Article in the Irish Independent 28th April 2007 by Dearbhail McDonal 'Immigration Bill targets "marriages of convenience"'.

10. Article in the Sunday Times 30th October 2016 by Mark Tighe 'Sham marriage probe voids 431 residency cards'.

11. Article in the Sunday Independent 11th January 2009 by Marc Coleman 'Migrants made 920,000 PPS number applications'.

12. Article in The Irish Times 12th August 2011 'EU allows restriction on right of Romanians to work in Spain'.

5 Implosion

1. See NCB Stockbrokers prediction in Appendix 6.

2. CSO press release 'This is Ireland – Highlights from Census 2011, Part 2

3. Article in the Sunday Independent 8th February 2009 by Louise McBride 'Permit crunch for foreign workers as dole numbers soar'

4. Opinion poll referred to in an article in the Irish Independent 24th January 2006 by Sam Smyth 'Fears over foreign workers coming here are misguided'.

5. Article in the Sunday Independent on 22nd January 2006 by Joseph O'Malley 'Immigration on election agenda after Rabbitte taps into politics of fear'.

6. Article in the Independent on 24th January 2006 by Sam Smyth 'Fears over foreign workers coming here are misguided'. See also Appendix 5.

6 The Welfare State

1. Article in the Irish Independent April 2004 by Nigel Morris and Stephen Castle 'Britain to curb benefits for new EU immigrants'.
2. Article in the Sunday Times 18th December 2011 by Stephen O'Brien 'Net tightens on welfare tourists'.
3. See page 58 paragraph 2
4. Article in the Sunday Times 4th September 2011 by Damien Kiberd 'Welfare gravy train must be derailed'.
5. Article in The Irish Times 20th November 2013 by Carl O'Brien
6. From an article in the Sunday Times 5th March 2017 by Stephen O'Brien 'Varadkar: cut child benefits going abroad'.
7. Article in The Irish Times 10th September 2008 by Ruadhan Mac Cormaic 'Tighter immigration policy favoured by 66% - poll'.

7 The Property Bubble

1. NCB Stockbrokers prediction on page 74
2. Article in the Irish Independent 29th November 2005 by Pat Boyle 'Migrants to boost Demand for houses'.
3. Article in the Irish Independent 25th January 2006 by Bill Tyson 'Influx of workers gives big boost to property'.
4. Article in the Irish Independent 24th January 2006 by Pat Boyle 'Let the good times roll on...'
5. Article in the Irish Independent 19th December 2006 by Pat Boyle 'Migrant workers push up growth ahead of EU rate'.
6. 6 Census 2011 Results Profile 4 "The Roof over our heads – Housing in Ireland"
7. See article in the Sunday Times 26th February 2016 by Mark Tighe 'Fine Gael heads the landlord list as TDs cash in with property'.

8 The Debate

1. Article in the Sunday Times 24th September 2017 by Eithne Shortall 'Women and young people are more negative on immigration'.
2. Article in The Irish Times 9th January 2016 by Breda O'Brien 'Finns could teach us a lesson on diversity in political discourse'.
3. Article in the Sunday Times 1st October 2017 by David Quinn 'It's not racist to have fears over immigration'.
4. See article in The Sun 17th November 2016 by Kieran Dineen
5. Article in the Sunday Independent 22nd January 2006 'Immigration on election agenda after Rabbitte taps into the politics of fear'.
6. Article in The Irish Times 10th September 2008 by Ruadhan MacCormaic 'Tighter immigration favoured by 66% - poll'.

9 Social Cohesion

1. Article in the Meath Chronicle 10th July 2018 by Paul Murphy 'Families get keys to new houses'.
2. Article in the Meath Chronicle 8th September 2018 by Ann Casey 'Council spending   €7.5m per year on HAP Scheme'
3. BBC News 17th October 2010 also Reuters
4. RTE News 10th January 2017.
5. UN International Migration Report 2017: Highlights page 28

10 The Law

1. Article in the Sunday Times 14th July 2013 by John Mooney 'Stubborn Moroccan costs the taxpayer €700,000
2. Article in the Sunday Times 9th July 2017 by Eithne Shortall '80% of failed asylum seekers stay'.
3. Article in The Irish Times 17th December 2010 by Jamie Smyth and Stephen Mangan 'Asylum seekers return after deportation plane breaks down'.

4. Article in the Sunday Times 21st July 2013 by Larissa Nolan '€2m cost of sending back 724 immigrants'.
5. Article in The Irish Times 22nd January 2010 by Mary Carolan 'Each bid to deport asylum seekers to go to court – judge'.
6. Article in the Sunday Times 3rd July 2011 by John Mooney 'Nigerian mother set to be deported'.
7. See Paul Colliers book 'Exodus' page 125
8. Article in the Sunday Times 2nd September 2018 by John Mooney 'Ireland used as backdoor into UK via reunified family ploy'.
9. Article in the Irish Independent 6th September 2008
10. Article in the Sunday Times 18th March 2018 by Mark Tighe 'Polish ministry's 'bias' pushes alleged Mafioso to seek asylum'.
11. Article in the Sunday Times 22nd December 2004 by Tom Brady 'A quarter of prison inmates are foreigners'.
12. Article in the Sunday Times 13th April 2014 by Mark Tighe 'Asylum seeker exposed as sex trafficker by prints'.
13. Article in the Irish Independent by Louise Hogan 'Call for stricter controls on number of foreign criminals entering the country'.

11 The Allure of a Better Life

1. See UN International Migration Report 2017 page 25
2. Article in The Irish Times on 22nd June 2017 by Paul Cullen 'Overseas doctors increase as Irish leave'.
3. See article in the Sunday Independent 6th May 2012 by Elaine Byrne 'IFSC living by its own rules and not in the real world'.

Appendix 1

An Central
Phríomh-Oifig Statistics
Staidrimh Office

Press Statement 📰

Preasráiteas

27 August 2019

Population and Migration Estimates April 2019

Population growth of 64,500 in the year to April 2019

- Ireland's usually resident population is estimated to be 4,921,500 in April 2019
- While 88,600 persons immigrated to Ireland in the year to April 2019, 26,900 (30.4%) of these were returning Irish nationals
- Of the 54,900 people who emigrated from Ireland in the year to April 2019, 29,000 (52.8%) were estimated to be Irish nationals
- Irish nationals experienced net outward migration of -2,100 persons, while net inward migration among non-Irish nationals was estimated to be +35,800 in the year to April 2019
- In April 2019, 622,700 non-Irish nationals were estimated to be resident in Ireland, accounting for 12.7% of the total population
- The population of Dublin in April 2019 was estimated to be almost 1.4 million persons, 28.4% of the total population

Go to release: Population and Migration Estimates April 2019

The Central Statistics Office (CSO) today (27 August 2019) publishes the annual Population and Migration Estimates for April 2019.

Appendix 1 page 2

Commenting, James Hegarty, Statistician said: "*The combined effect of positive net migration and sustained natural increase resulted in population growth of 64,500 (+1.3%) in the year to April 2019. This annual increase brings the population estimate to 4.92 million in April 2019.*

The number of immigrants to the State in the year to April 2019 is estimated to be 88,600, while the number of emigrants from the State over the same period is estimated at 54,900. These flows resulted in net inward migration for Ireland in the year to April 2019 of +33,700. The number of births in the year to April 2019 was 61,200 while the number of deaths was 30,400, resulting in a natural increase of +30,800.

In the year to April 2019, Irish nationals accounted for 26,900 (30.4%) of the 88,600 immigrants to Ireland and 29,000 (52.8%) of the 54,900 emigrants from Ireland. Consequently, net outward migration of Irish nationals in 2019 was -2,100. This represents a decrease of 2,200 on 2018 when net inward migration of Irish nationals was estimated to be +100 persons.

In the year to April 2019, 61,700 non-Irish nationals arrived to live in Ireland and 25,900 non-Irish nationals emigrated abroad. Therefore, net inward migration among non-Irish nationals remained strong and was estimated to be +35,800 in 2019. These positive inflows resulted in the number of non-Irish nationals living in Ireland increasing from 593,600 persons in April 2018 to 622,700 persons in April 2019, accounting for 12.7% of the total population.

All regions showed a population increase in the year to April 2019, ranging from 2,600 persons (0.5%) in the Mid-West to 25,100 persons (1.8%) in Dublin. Consequently, the population of Dublin in April 2019 was estimated to be almost 1.4 million persons, equating to 28.4% of the total population."

For further information contact:

James Hegarty (+353) 21 453 5429 or Caroline Barrett (+353) 21 453 5485

or email demography@cso.ie

-- ENDS --

Appendix 2   page 1

5 April 2004

Mr Frank Cosgrove

Dear Mr. Cosgrove,

Thank you for your letter which, despite its many insulting comments and derogatory tone, raises a few interesting points.

If allowing workers from the new member states access to Ireland turns out to be the "disastrous policy" you fear, it is open to the Government to change that policy. There is no evidence to show that current policy will result in migrant workers flooding the Irish labour market. It is also very important to appreciate the substantial contribution migrant worker have already made to our economy and society. We will continue to need this contribution in the future.

On the specific issue of labour substitution, Congress and our affiliated unions have been involved in lengthy discussions with the Department of Enterprise, Trade and Employment to agree policies and procedures aimed at protecting the jobs of Irish workers. We believe it is possible to do this without locking out workers from other EU countries. Irish workers and Irish society have benefited greatly from having access to other countries in the past and continue to do so.

We are well aware of the pressures on the lives of working people and their families caused by the lack of adequate housing, hospitals, schools and other infrastructures. Congress is involved in intensive negotiating and lobbying to have our social services and general infrastructure improved and developed. Our efforts in this important area have met with varying degrees of success. For example, the initiative on affordable housing which we negotiated as part of Sustaining Progress should deliver a home for ten thousand young couples.

You rightly state the job that trade union members are paying us for is "protecting wages and conditions". The wage increases which we negotiate are voted on by union members in democratic ballots. It is the members who decide whether the increases are adequate. Protecting the value of wage increases involves dealing with other issues like taxation and inflation while protecting conditions involves a wide range of provisions from pensions and holidays to child care and healthy work environments.

31-32 Parnell Square, Dublin 1, Ireland

Tel. 353 1 889 7777   Fax: 353 1 887 2012

Email: congress@ictu.ie   Web site: www.ictu.ie

Affiliated to the European Trade Union Confederation   General Secretary: David Begg

Appendix 2   page 2

As far as your complaint about 'pet projects' is concerned, campaigning for equality for all workers, irrespective of nationality, is not some optional 'add on' for Congress. It is spelled out very clearly in our constitution under OBJECTS OF CONGRESS parg. (b):

"To ensure full equality in all aspects of employment opportunity and to oppose discrimination on any such grounds as colour, ethnic or national origins ,politics, race, religion, sex, age and disability."

Congress will continue to oppose discrimination and fight for equal employment opportunities for all workers while remaining vigilant to the danger of some employers using 'foreign' workers as cheap labour to displace indigenous workers.

Yours sincerely

David Begg
GENERAL SECRETARY

db/es

Appendix 3

Article in the Irish Independent 26th November 2005

Industrial showdown looms as row places social partnership in danger

**Senan Molony
and Ralph Riegel**

THE Irish Ferries row could be the rock on which social partnership perishes, TDs warned last night.

Labour leader Pat Rabbitte said the entire Irish trade union movement was united in fighting the unfair disposal of Irish workers and their replacement with cut-price foreign labour.

"This is a huge issue not just for the Irish Ferries workers but for the entire labour movement," he said.

Meanwhile, Socialist party TD Joe Higgins said the Taoiseach's "white flag of surrender" had given the go-ahead for what he said were Irish Ferries' bullyboy tactics.

Bertie Ahern's recent remarks that "nothing could be done" about the plan to replace 543 workers with cheaper labour had given the green light to the company in the action it had taken in Pembroke and Holyhead, he said.

Despite some words of criticism, by its failure to act the Government was showing that its real sympathy was with the drive to maximise profits at the expense of wages and conditions, he added, calling the issue "a life or death challenge to the trade union movement as a whole".

Mr Rabbitte warned that if Irish Ferries were allowed swap Irish workers for cheaper East European contract labour, similar actions would be undertaken by employers in the construction, services and manufacturing sectors.

"We all know the consequences of that for Irish workers and families," he said.

It was extraordinary that an Irish company should revert to "SAS-style tactics" in dealing with their workers, Mr Rabbitte said.

Now every trade union in Ireland was watching the outcome of the Irish Ferries stand-off.

Mr Rabbitte said that after the Taoiseach made a recent declaration of his socialism and then promised to do all in his powers to resolve the Irish Ferries dispute, "Bertie Ahern effectively walked away and cleared the way for the firm's tough tactics".

The Taoiseach said yesterday, however, that the attitude of the company was anathema to everything he had worked for over 20 years. Irish Ferries were "trying to turn back the clock" and should even now reconsider its actions.

Appendix 4

Article in the Irish Independent 4th April 2004

Harney's riled by top tax man's jibe over Irish rates

MARTIN FITZPATRICK

THE Tanaiste Mary Harney said yesterday she was "amazed" at the comment from leading Dublin tax accountant Paul McGowan which suggested that Ireland should think of raising the corporation tax rates.

Ms Harney said she knew Mr McGowan, KPMG's senior tax partner, but "I'm amazed he would make comments like this". She said the growth in the Irish economy was built on the back of low tax rates and there was "no question of throwing in the towel".

"We have allies in Europe who think the same way about low taxes and I am confident that we will win the debate," she said.

Mary Harney wasn't the only one to bristle at McGowan's suggestions at a conference in Dublin in the middle of the week. The IDA was said to be "up in arms" over the remarks which were taken as unhelpful in the midst of the tax debate that is linked with the development of a new Constitution for the EU.

Commenting to the *Sunday Independent* yesterday Paul McGowan said he was in favour of Ireland retaining a veto on tax changes. But in his scripted remarks earlier in the week he said the country should debate "whether it is time for Ireland to reconsider its position on tax harmonisation".

Rightly guessing that his comments could "sound like national treason" he said Ireland could avoid future questioning of its tax rates by the high-tax states by grabbing the initiative itself. He suggested Ireland could contemplate a future with a 15 per cent corporate tax rate, along with a "guarantee that for 25 years we were the lowest rate in the EU".

"Perhaps we need to reconsider our attitudes to tax harmonisation and realise that our opposition to it was a means to an end and not an end itself," McGowan added.

Fears over foreign workers coming here are misguided

SAM SMYTH

THE race-to-the-bottom might represent a new low for politics but it would ultimately place a nuclear depth charge in the heart of the Irish economy.

Last week's opinion polls showed that kindling the fears of an historically insecure workforce paid electoral dividends for the Labour Party.

But the accumulated wisdom of the economists and others who have studied the potential of our future say we need another 300,000 foreign workers over the next 10 years. That's if Ireland's unique economic success is to be maintained, and even accelerated, we have to encourage more, not less, workers to sell their labour here.

Still, while talk of work permits for foreigners promises an electoral bonanza, it was obvious that some might try to make hay.

So, no one should be too surprised when Ned O'Keeffe intervened to claim some of the anti-immigrant sentiment for Fianna Fáil.

Both Pat Rabbitte and Ned O'Keeffe used the word 'anecdotal' in their evidence to support those Irish workers who felt threatened by foreign workers.

However, 'anecdotal' is the sort of loaded word that somehow sounds grand but could actually be said better by 'a fella told me in a pub'.

Feeding on the irrational fears of historically insecure workers is an extremely dangerous and irresponsible pitch for those who should know better.

There is a ready made market of anti-immigrant xenophobes prepared to use the politicians' respectability as currency for their prejudice. Any party, or politicians, who can harness the fear-of-foreigners vote can expect a corresponding electoral bonus.

Pat Rabbitte's personal rating jumped by four per cent. And the Labour Party's two per cent increase, in last week's TNS MRBI poll was delivered after raising the question of work permits for foreign workers.

Within days, Ned O'Keeffe relayed the fears of his constituents about the same foreign workers.

Which begs the question: Would Pat Rabbitte or Ned O'Keeffe have spoken about foreign workers so candidly had those workers been Africans rather than east Europeans?

Neither Rabbitte nor O'Keeffe is either racist or xenophobe: they are decent men articulating real fears apparently held by four out of every five Irish people, according to an opinion poll. Yet while they have an obligation to ventilate the genuinely held fears of their constituents, there is an even greater responsibility to calm irrational views.

There is too much at stake for anyone to seek electoral gain from such a potentially destructive hypothesis.

The trade unions, particularly SIPTU, attached a pair of jump leads to the Irish Ferries dispute and tapped into a deep-seated fear.

Irish workers feared that their wages and working conditions would be undercut by an influx of workers from predominately east European EU countries.

And that those immigrants would be prepared to work for less money in sweat shops thus dragging down the pay and conditions the native Irish had negotiated their way above over a generation.

The trade union movement represents maybe 25pc of the workforce and as much as 80pc of those are employed in the public sector. If those immigrants are not signing up for trade union membership, the leadership might see their long term future threatened.

However, the real political business is to be done in the upcoming round of pay talks with the government. Bertie Ahern is seeking his three-in-a-row as Taoiseach and will listen sympathetically to the unions.

Pat Rabbitte's intervention on the union's side under the ugly word 'displacement' will allow him to claim some credit if, or rather when, a deal is done.

Kindling the fears of an historically insecure workforce paid electoral dividends

Migrants to boost demand for houses

Pat Boyle

THE arrival of 11,000 migrant workers a month will keep demand for new houses at record levels.

The house market will be buoyant for the next 15 years, a new study from NCB Stockbrokers predicts.

The report says that demand for new houses is still on the rise and is forecast to reach up to 75,000 a year for the next decade-and-a-half.

The brokers say that population growth and the arrival of migrant workers will continue to drive up demand for new homes.

"The continuing rise in the over-25 population provides a strong base for housing demand," the report states. And it highlights immigration as the key to sustaining the current pace of house completions.

NCB believe that immigration is likely to accelerate because of the freedom of access granted to citizens of the 10 new EU countries.

And they say that increasing income and levels of wealth are supporting investment in the existing housing stock and in second homes.

The brokers estimate that more than 10,000 second homes are being constructed each year and they believe that demand for new housing units could reach 75,000 a year between now and 2021. However, this assumes inward migration of 75,000 a year as well as a reduction in the average household size.

After rising at about 4pc in the first half of this year, house price inflation reached 10pc in the third quarter of this year and the report says these soaring house prices are helping borrowers.

Inflation

NCB quote an example of a 90pc mortgage taken out to buy an averagely priced house in 2003. Two years later this would stand at just 67pc of the house's value.

And even though house price inflation is slowing and interest rates are rising, NCB predicts that a similar 90pc mortgage taken out this year will amount to 69pc of the house value by 2009.

The report says the rise in debt in Ireland is .not a problem because of the borrower's ability to repay.

NCB state that mortgage repayments are estimated to be about 31pc of disposable income in 2005 and even if interest rates rise to 4pc, this percentage would still be less than 35pc of disposable income.

80% of failed asylum seekers stay

Eithne Shortall

Just 20% of deportation orders for unsuccessful asylum seekers are estimated to be implemented in Ireland, according to a report published by the Economic and Social Research Institute (ESRI).

The report, which was produced for the European Migration Network (EMN), said it was impossible to give an exact implementation rate, as some orders might be enforced years after they were issued, but that approximately 80% of deportation judgements were believed to go unimplemented.

An EMN report found that Ireland was unusual within the European Union because it allowed rejected asylum seekers to continue residing in direct provision accommodation. The rejected applicants retain their medical cards, which provide access to all public medical services in the state, children can continue to

Asylum seekers protest at Mosney camp, Co Meath

attend school, and they "can also continue to receive some exceptional needs payment".

This did not match the general trend within the EU of "moving towards a policy of reducing material supports available to rejected asylum seekers in order to disincentivise stay and to encourage co-operation with return procedures".

The ESRI found that the focus of public debate in Ireland was not on the return of rejected asylum seekers

but rather on the humanitarian issues surrounding the migration crisis and how Ireland was responding to it. A review of parliamentary debates in the Dáil indicated that the non-return of rejected applicants was not a focus. However, "effective return is still a priority for Irish policymakers".

Other factors contributing to the low implementation rate of deportation orders are the weak relationships

between Ireland and the countries to which they are deporting – many do not have embassies here – and a High Court judgment dating from 2013.

In the case of Omar vs the Governor of Cloverhill Prison, it was decided that the state had no legislative power to enter a private dwelling to enforce a deportation order. "This challenge was common to all deportation orders, not just those in respect of rejected asylum seekers," said the ESRI report. However, legislation introduced in 2015 allowed the Garda National Immigration Bureau to enter a home for the purpose of arrest relating to a deportation order.

Other obstacles to implementation include "evasion of deportation orders, judicial reviews taken by persons subject to deportation orders, and the impact of a 'trailing family member' at another stage in the protection process".